WE'RE LIVING THROUGH THE

BREAK DOWN

AND HERE'S WHAT WE CAN DO ABOUT IT

Elliott&Thompson

First published 2019 by
Elliott and Thompson Limited
2 John Street, London WC1N 2ES
www.eandtbooks.com

This paperback edition first published in 2020

ISBN: 978-1-78396-497-0

9 8 7 6 5 4 3 2 1

A catalogue record for this book is available from the British Library.

Typesetting by Marie Doherty
Printed by CPI Group (UK) Ltd, Croydon, CR0 4YY

For Caitlin, Alfred and Felix

Contents

Introduction

In the deepest, darkest depths of history, there was once a time when most families had only one screen in their house. It was in a room where everyone would come together to fight about which of the three, four or five channels they would watch. This forced people into a situation in which they would have to compromise. Imagine the horror.

One consequence of those days, though, was that people used to watch the news together. Possibly because *Casualty* had just finished and *Match of the Day* was yet to begin, but still, it happened. And when people watch the news together, it sparks conversation. Of course, nobody ever agrees with their parents, so sometimes those conversations would escalate into arguments. Your views on a particular news story might have been challenged. Maybe you would have changed your mind. Probably not. But at least you'd have heard the other side of the argument.

Jump forward to today. Everyone has their own screen. We all receive our news from our own chosen sources. When we see a story, it is often pre-filtered for our approval ('You won't believe what the prime minister has done today . . .'). When we see it, we can share it with our friends, who already tend to agree with us. We're all operating within our own echo chambers, constantly having our views confirmed, applauded, reinforced. Like a sports fan determined to keep their head down so they won't find out the final score before catching the match highlights, we actively choose not to look at the other side.

Here's an example. In the run-up to the 2018 local elections, there was much talk that there would be huge Labour gains. This was Corbyn Time. Cometh the hour, cometh the man. High fives all round. All that stuff.

In the event, Labour did make gains of 3 per cent and the Conservatives did make some losses – roughly 3 per cent. But, overall, the Conservative vote appeared to have been largely held up by an almost total collapse of the UKIP vote.

When it came to reporting on these figures, though, the echo-chamber effect was very clear. Guido Fawkes reported the results as 'Bad night for Labour, Tories hold London Councils and make gains across England'. Skwawkbox looked at exactly the same data and led with 'Labour had its best local election results in London since 1971 – almost fifty years – and its second-best ever.' How you receive news matters because it shapes your perception of events. It walls you into your box.

The trouble is, we've shown that we actually rather like our news in this form. How much easier is it to have everything ready-made for us to enjoy, away from the tempestuous sea of political arguments, where our views might be challenged? We've constructed our pillow forts with the greatest of care and attention. We're safe from any uneasy doubts that might sneak in, any notion that we could be wrong about something.

This is so much the case that there is now an entire industry based on getting you fired up.

Partisan sites like 'Westmonster' or 'The Canary' exist purely on subscriptions from their audience. Often these sites don't even try to pretend that they are presenting impartial news. Sure, media outlets, especially newspapers, have always tended to lean one way or the other, but it didn't used to be quite so in-your-face. It's like how the Joker sometimes wears make-up to fit in, until suddenly he doesn't. In our current political climate, the Joker is in full hideous view, asking us 'Why so serious?'

So, these subscription 'news' websites have a vested interest in keeping you angry. If you are only mildly distracted by how bad something is, you're likely to shake your head a little and then get on with your life. But if you're furious, if you feel like you can't just sit there and let this stuff happen, you're more likely to subscribe to these sites. You'll feel like your money will help in the Good Fight to uphold your ideals and values.

Reinforcing and encouraging people's views like this can lead them to believe that their opinion is not just different, but better – that they have pedigree opinions. Points of view they would show off in whatever the debating version of

Crufts might be. Standing proudly by as the judge circulates, before walking their opinion around a course (presumably made up of pub, dinner-party and social-media sections). If their opinion does not win 'Best in Show', they'll be furious. Just imagine the Twitter storm they'll create, blasting all the other competitors.

And here we find the problem. The demonisation of everyone else. The creation of memes and other 'shareable' content that does nothing but be mean and abusive about the other side. If you're on social media, you'll have seen them – unfortunate pictures of politicians with captions that ask how we can possibly trust them, or that point out how stupid the opposition leaders, MPs or activists are.

As I write, there is one doing the rounds on both sides of the divide. It shows someone's brain being replaced with dog poo and they then shout out some sort of ridiculous comment. Images like this are then shared hundreds, maybe thousands of times. The more you see this sort of thing, the harder it becomes to take that person seriously. Every time they open their mouth, you think of that absurd meme plastered across the internet. They are permanently marked down as stupid/uncaring/selfish. It's so easy and so cheap and so destructive. And every time we share a meme, picture or article that confirms our righteous decisions and opinions, we deepen that division; we create a narrative of 'them' and 'us'; we dehumanise the opposition. And we prevent any kind of meaningful debate.

All of which has led us to The Breakdown. The breakdown

of communication. The breakdown of understanding. The breakdown in trust.

What makes this so sad is that modern-day politics is more complex than ever. We live in a world where corporations are multinational, where migration waves are global and climate change edges the entire world into unchartered territory. Yet, here we are, trying to find solutions to these global issues on our small rock off the coast of Europe, while at the same time trying to deal with our own national problems. We've got children living in poverty, homeless people on our streets, the elderly choosing between heating and eating. We all agree that these are problems, and yet it's not easy to find solutions that we can all agree on. This isn't rearranging the deckchairs on the *Titanic*. This is arguing about suggested plans for the formation of the deckchairs while water laps at their feet.

You see, politics matters. It's just hugely important. All these issues need sorting out and in order to do so, people need to come together, with their many different ideas and potential solutions, and find a way to communicate, to compromise.

I do a live show – a comedy politics thing – aimed at children and families. We start by asking the audience what the fairest way would be to split eight sweets between ten children. They come up with a few suggestions, we talk about them for a bit, then everyone votes for their preferred solution. They often decide that if not everyone can have a sweet, nobody should have one. That seems to be the general feeling among six- to twelve-year-olds. Although we've had some other pretty amazing suggestions too: licking the sweets and passing them on; fighting for the sweets; and even burning them. Anyway, the point of this scenario is to show how politics works, how democracy works, and what effect it can have. Put simply: problem – solutions – debate – vote – action. That's it. That's politics.

Except that doesn't seem to be the way people are doing things these days. We're living through The Breakdown. When there is a problem in our country – and there are many – it's much more usual for people to get angry that the problem exists, to scream about whose fault it is, to shout louder than anyone else so alternative viewpoints can't be heard or discussed, and to resort to insults rather than engaging in debate.

At a time when politics so badly needs solutions, we're not interested in calmly identifying the problem and discussing a range of possible options that everyone can agree on. It's my way or the highway. I'm right, you're wrong. It's tearing us apart.

By 2018, both leaders of the two major parties had faced votes of no confidence from within their parties, Jeremy Corbyn in 2016, Theresa May in 2018. Both saw off their challengers, but it shows that even people who describe themselves as Conservative or Labour supporters can't agree with each other on the general direction of travel for their own party, let alone have constructive conversations with the other side. In February 2019, the disagreements got so bad a number of MPs left both the Conservative Party and the Labour Party. Groupings that used to be broad churches are becoming fractured and narrow.

Imagine trying to live your life this way. Imagine trying to plan a night in with friends – people who you've chosen to live with because you supposedly share a similar outlook on life – picking out a takeaway and a series on Netflix. But rather than calmly discussing the options to work out what suits the tastes of the wider group, you're hellbent on stating your own, slightly left-field, preferences and refusing to listen to anyone else. At best you end up a bit lonely, one of you stranded with pizza, *The Good Place* and regret in one room, while it's a Chinese, *Stranger Things* and floods of tears in another. At worst? Nobody watches or eats anything. The room is set on fire. The building burns down.

And who loses out? We all do. But especially the most vulnerable people in our society, the ones who need the government the most. It makes it hard to move forward on even simple things, let alone the complex mess of something like Brexit.

The Breakdown has caused such a huge rift, it's evident in our daily lives. In April 2018, there was a demonstration on the beach in my hometown. Fishermen were protesting about being kept under EU fishing rules during the transition period. They had voted Leave partly because they had been told they would be free of the rules that they say discriminate against them. Nigel Farage came down, along with another former UKIP leader, Henry Bolton. With such prestigious guests, there was a counter-protest from Liberal Democrat- and Labour-voting Remain campaigners.

I went down to take some pictures and report on the protest. The whole thing was utterly miserable. Both sides were so completely engrossed in their own perspectives, they just looked at the other side and shook their heads. Occasionally, people tried to convert each other, but they had no chance because neither side was listening. That's how it is in communities blighted by The Breakdown. Different sides, all amazed at the awfulness of the other, unable to communicate, to make informed decisions for the good of the community, to understand each other – unwilling even to try. Remember that room that was burning down because of your culinary and televisual preferences? Well, on this occasion they did literally set a boat on fire. One huge burning metaphor for politics in The Breakdown.

It's not just face-to-face that we see these issues. Online, especially on social media, abuse is all around us. I run an organisation called Simple Politics. I don't like to go on about it, but it's pretty great. (For transparency reasons I should tell you that this is not even vaguely true: I love talking about Simple Politics. If you ever have the misfortune to be sat next to me on the train, you will hear a constant barrage of Interesting Things from SP. Sorry, not sorry.)

The aim of Simple Politics is to be non-partisan, clear and vaguely light-hearted, and I'm proud to say that our little corner of social media is generally populated by lovely people. We don't do the 'making you angry' thing; that's partly the point – we're trying to inform without taking sides. But even so, some of the comments people post are vile. Of course, for me it's a simple matter of banning them and reporting them if necessary. Out there, though, on the high seas of social media, it's much worse and more widespread. You've seen it, I'm sure. In 2018, Theresa May said 'As well as being places for empowering self-expression, online platforms can become places of intimidation and abuse . . . This squanders the opportunity new technology affords us to drive up political engagement and can have the perverse effect of putting off participation from those who are not prepared to tolerate the levels of abuse which exist.' It's something experienced by literally everyone who tries to enter into debate, from the grassiest of grass roots, to the top of the tree.

And so, it is here that we find ourselves. This book is about taking a step back. Taking a moment to listen and understand other people. Finding out where they're coming from. Realising that just because someone has a different opinion to you, that doesn't necessarily make them wrong. Or a Nazi.

'How are we going to do that?' I hear you ask. We're going to do it together. We're going to take a guided tour around UK politics. We'll get off the bus at a few key stops, maybe buy a sandwich, use the facilities, before getting back on and continuing on our way.

The first proper stop on The Breakdown bus is at the major ideologies in UK politics. Finding out how people think and why, what their priorities are, and how they all arrive at such opposing ideas and solutions.

Once we've got the hang of the ideologies, we'll stop off to have some squash, maybe a slice of cake, while we take a look at some of the main disputes of the day. To really understand the alternative points of view, you have to look at specific issues. We'll look at seven battlefields, such as privatisation, free speech and gender. These examples will really show you why people think differently to you – not necessarily that they are right and you're wrong, or vice versa, just that they think about things in another way.

There won't be a comprehensive breakdown of every single issue. That's not the point. This isn't a textbook from which you can look up each side of every argument for every topic. No, this is a springboard, a way to get started. You'll see how it works, how these political battlefields fall down ideological lines. You've probably already noticed it happening everywhere. From interviews on TV to arguments down the pub, these ideological battlefields are all around us. But, hopefully, now you'll start to understand where everyone is coming from. And that it's OK to disagree.

So, by that point on our tour, we'll get it. We'll understand other people, even if we don't agree with them. Our conversations will be busting The Breakdown.

Except you're not really interested in politics just to understand other people. You're interested in politics so that you can start to make the world look a bit more like you want it to look, right? So, Part Three of this book is about change-makers. These are the people who have been passionate about a cause and have played a pivotal role in making change happen. There are a range of people (and animals), from Nigel Farage to Finn the dog. You might not agree with everything they've done, but I hope you'll find the stories of their efforts and campaigns inspirational and thought provoking, better preparing you for life in The Breakdown.

Finally, because we've got an idiosyncratic political system that has its own quirks and foibles, at the back of the book you'll find a look at the mechanics of UK politics, how it all works. If you're going to be able to stand on your own two feet out there, you've got to know where you stand – with the constitution, with government, with Parliament and with the local representatives too. Don't worry, you don't need a politics degree to understand it all, this is just some of the basics. Most of us weren't taught this stuff at school, so there is no shame in not knowing it. And a lot of it is shrouded in mystery and jargon, some of which can get pretty complicated, but I'll make it as painless as possible. Promise.

That said, if you know your way around, if you're something of a whizz already, don't worry about those pages. They're there if you'd like to know more, but aren't crucial to removing yourself from The Breakdown.

Alas, after that, we must go our separate ways. This is only a book. As we part, though, have a look around. You'll notice the difference. Sure, The Breakdown is still going on around you, but you'll be able to see through some of the bluster, to communicate with people with whom you disagree – you can be part of the solution.

PART ONE

How Other People Think

The first step in making sense of UK politics is to understand why people say and do things you disagree with. It's so easy to look around and be completely dumbfounded at the evilness of other people. It seems so obvious that they've got it wrong, why can't they see it? The reality is very simple: people just think differently to you. To understand, we need to start by looking at the various political ideologies.

An ideology is a joined-up way of looking at politics. You have some key principles and you stick to them. That means everything has to fit around them. It's like when you were sixteen and you had that prized pair of Reebok trainers – other people might not have been that into them (trust me, they weren't), but you were. They were what everything else had to work around. That's how ideologies tend to work. People put freedom or equality or animal liberation, or whatever, front and centre. Everything else falls in line with that.

It's really important to understand that it's not just politics that are shaped by ideologies. It's an alternative way of thinking. It affects the way people see every aspect of their lives. Let's look at an example of how deep-rooted these perspectives on life can be. Now, it is unlikely you're reading this with a glass of mulled wine in your hand and East 17 ringing in your ears; you're just as likely to be on the bus on a rainy Tuesday in March. But for a very simple way of looking at how ideology affects every part of life, allow me to get festive and think about Christmas.

Liberals and libertarians: Liberals are all about freedom, plurality and diversity. That's exactly how they see Christmas: a festival of celebration, whether you're enjoying Christmas, Hanukkah or even Saturnalia. Liberals are happy there are decent TV, presents, good food and the opportunity to chase your personal vision of happiness.

Socialists: Socialists aren't huge fans of religion. It is hierarchical and distracts from the human condition. That doesn't mean they don't like Christmas – they're all about the giving and the human kindness part, and the strengthening of community bonds. Just don't expect a present from Amazon.

Conservatives: Conservatives love tradition and family. That makes Christmas day pretty big for them. Church. Turkey. No presents until after the Queen's Speech.

One-nation conservatives/social democrats: This lot occupy the middle ground. They like traditions – in fact, anything done on Christmas Day could become a tradition that has to be stuck with for years – but are accepting of other people's customs as well. They're slightly uncomfortable with the rampant consumerism but join in nonetheless.

If something as seemingly simple as Christmas can attract so many different opinions from across the ideologies, what does that tell us about more obviously 'political' issues? Ideologies are inescapable, and they can be quite complex. What you are about to read is a very brief overview of their main principles. If you are interested in finding out more, there are some very detailed books written by people who are considerably cleverer than me. I find them a little dull.

Free-market economics

Now, you may, quite rightly, have expected this section to start by looking at an ideology. That's what this whole chunk of book is supposed to be about. Ideologies. Before we get there, though, we need to have a look at the free market. It's vital to understanding what's to come.

The principle of free-market economics is that we are all free to do whatever we like to earn money and, once it's been earned, we are all free to spend it on whatever we like. Nobody can tell you how much to spend on anything, nor how much you can charge for anything. You can set the price you want and if people are interested in what you are selling, at the cost you are selling it, they will buy it. This is all thanks to supply and demand.

Supply is how many people want to sell a thing, at one price or another. Let's take something we can all get behind: pictures of cats looking cute. Yes. Cat memes. Imagine for a second that we had to pay to view cat memes. Now, if anyone producing cat memes could make, say, £1,000 for every cat meme they created, there would be a lot of people who would want to get into the cat-meme creation game. A whole lot of people. On the other hand, if you could only sell your work for 1p, there would be a lot fewer people who would be up for it. Almost none.

The profit motive means that the more that can be charged for something, the more people want to be involved in selling it. Sure, some people would be in the market because they just really love funny pictures of cats. Many, many more, though, would jump on the bus for the money they can make.

Demand is how many people want to buy the product. When it comes to demand, if a cat meme was to set you back a grand, not that many people would buy one. All those sellers would be sorely disappointed. Alternatively, millions of people might sign up to buy their cat memes for 1p. There would be a stampede. Unfortunately, though, there would be hardly anybody selling them. It would be too hard to make a living from such a tiny return.

Somewhere in the middle there is a meeting point. A price at which a reasonable number of people want to sell and a reasonable amount of people want to buy. That point is the equilibrium. Nobody sets the equilibrium. We all just work it out as we go along. An economist called Adam Smith referred to this as the 'invisible hand' that guides us.

To give a more personal example, I run an organisation called Simple Politics. I often do talks, school visits and events. At some point when setting up these things, I'm asked how much I charge. And it's a nightmare. I can calculate what my overheads are, what transport to the area might cost, maybe accommodation, what else I would have to turn down in order to do this, and so on, but at the end of the day, it comes down to what the buyer is prepared to pay.

If the price I come up with is too high, they won't book me. Or at least they'll negotiate me down. If the price I come up with is too low, I'm missing out on money that the organisation desperately needs and, ultimately, I'm threatening the existence of the whole darn project. Between us, we need to find a price that we're both happy with. If that's not possible, no booking will take place.

That's the economic argument, but it is a little more complicated than that. Just like those cat-meme enthusiasts, I love talking about politics. If something is exciting and relatively local, I may well do it for less than the price equilibrium. This shows us two things: 1) even the concept of price equilibrium is flexible, and we are free to respond to it as we wish, and 2) I'm terrible at business.

That's how the whole supply-and-demand thing works. And it is very flexible. If there is only one person selling a product, they can keep the price a bit higher. A bottle of Coke might be more expensive on the platform of a train station than it is in any other shop. That's because there is only one vendor you have access to if you fancy a caffeinated sugary soft drink. On the high street, though, there will be many places, so they are in competition with each other. That drives the price down.

For people who like the free market, one of its main draws is that we all benefit from people acting in their own self-interest. The town I live in didn't used to have a Mexican restaurant. People used to comment that they'd love to have somewhere they could buy a burrito. Then, when the bank closed, someone chose to open a Mexican restaurant there instead. Nobody forced them. It was their decision, in their own self-interest. Once the Mexican restaurant opened, people could eat there, or they could not eat there. If the food is good and it's reasonably priced, people are likely to go. They will choose to spend their money at this restaurant. And if they do that, the restaurant owner makes money. Everyone benefits, but everyone is acting in their own self-interest.

Flexibility is another bonus for fans of the free market. With so few rules, things can change very quickly. I was vegan in the late 1990s when it was pretty niche. Soya milk was expensive and could only be bought in health food shops. There was one café in Soho that used to do soya cappuccinos. Now? Veganism is much more widespread and so there is a huge variety of cheap soya milk readily available and sold in almost every café. The market for soya milk has completely changed. That's supply and demand right there.

The final example I want to look at here is something very close to my heart: beer. Specifically, beer in pubs. You will have noticed over the past few years that there has been an explosion in craft beer. This trend is only possible because some people are prepared to pay considerably more for a pint. On my high street there is a craft beer pub about 150 yards from a JD Wetherspoons. At one you'll pay over a fiver for a beer and at the other you'll pay around £2. Both pubs are successful businesses. Some people choose to pay more, some choose to pay less. Some will go to both. Others will choose different places, maybe somewhere that shows the football or has live music. The market offers a wide variety of choice and the consumer pays their money and makes their choice.

This free market now operates on a global scale. We buy and sell things around the world. That means you no longer need to have a relationship with the ultimate consumer of your product. A Mexican farmer doesn't need to know that avocado on toast is a popular snack in the UK, they only need to know that the price for which they can sell an avocado has gone up. That might mean they'll swap their tomato plants for avocados, which in turn increases the number of avocados produced and those trendy cafes in Shoreditch will have their supply needs met.

Ladies and gentlemen, that's all the time we've got at the Free Market stop on this tour. We're off to check out some actual ideologies now. If you were hoping to spend a bit more time here, don't worry. All the ideologies have pretty strong opinions about the free market – and that should help us to understand where they're coming from.

Liberalism

Like Mel Gibson in *Braveheart*, liberalism is all about freedom. Freedom to do what you would like to do. Freedom to be who you want to be. Freedom to express yourself in any way you wish.

To say that liberals like freedom is something of an understatement. They blooming love it. I hope very much that at some point in my life I will love something the way that liberals love freedom.

If you need proof, let's look at some of the founding ideas for liberalism. It has its roots in the seventeenth century but it didn't really start to become a big thing until the 1700s. At that point, there were all kinds of feudal and hierarchical arrangements in place, and most people had very little individual liberty. But in the late 1700s, times started to change. The Americans rose up against their British overlords for one. What did their Declaration of Independence call for in 1776? Yep. Freedom. Specifically, the right to 'Life, Liberty and the pursuit of Happiness'. Remember the bit in the free market section about people acting in their own self-interest? That's all about the belief that society is better off if we all act in 'pursuit' of our own version of 'Happiness'.

It wasn't just the Americans that were all over this. The French Revolution began not long after, in 1789. The next year, one of its leaders, Maximilien Robespierre, coined a phrase that would become synonymous with the revolution and that is still the national motto of France: 'Liberté, égalité, fraternité'. That's freedom, equality and brotherhood. What comes first? Freedom. At the time of the revolution, the phrase was also often followed by 'ou la mort', which means 'or death'. Freedom or death.

To be fair, both the American Declaration of Independence and the French motto also refer to equality, and that's a key part of the ideology too. But what that equality means is something that liberals have argued about. A lot. And we will come back to this a bit later.

Before we leave the eighteenth century altogether, though, it's worth having a look at what else was happening at that time. Adam Smith (remember him? He was the 'invisible hand' guy we spoke about a few pages ago) was busy writing the template for liberal economics. His book *The Wealth of Nations* was published in 1776, the same year as the Americans were calling for their liberty. The links between liberalism and the free market are there for everyone to see.

Anyway. This isn't a history lesson. It just helps to understand that liberalism and the desire for freedom has been around for quite a long time. Also, that it has always been inherently linked to capitalism.

So, how does this work? On a day-to-day basis it works around the free market. Everyone is free to act in the way they desire. In doing so they create a society or community with those around them. That's what almost all liberals would agree on.

The issue is what happens when this goes wrong. What happens when people need more support? How does that sit with the importance of freedom?

The answer lies in what kind of freedom you believe in. There's the idea of 'freedom from' and 'freedom to'. 'Freedom from' means that you are free from all state interference and rules. It might be the first one you think of. The kind of freedom that people in prison might dream of. It's not a complicated idea – you're free to do anything you want as long as it doesn't have a negative impact on other people. While liberals disagree on the extent of that freedom, a truly liberal government might take some steps to have fewer things banned and leave people to make their own decisions.

So, you are free to make money in whatever way you see fit and you are free to spend that money in whatever way you see fit. You don't have to work, but then you will struggle to pay for nice things. It's your choice whether to leave school early and start making money, or to stay on, learn a bit more and then maybe earn more later on. You want to drink yourself into the gutter? No worries, my friend. Just don't expect us to pull you out.

The legalisation of drugs, for example, is a typically liberal idea. It should be up to us what we put into our body. Yes, there are negative effects of drug use, but who makes decisions about me? Me, that's who. The other advantage of legalising drugs is that the free market will regulate the trade. Cost, purity, user experience and all that will be controlled by the invisible hand.

Don't forget, though, most liberals who believe in 'free from' still believe in restricting liberty where individuals might harm one another. There aren't big liberal movements to allow greater access to knives or guns. Not in the UK, anyway. While liberals may campaign against online restrictions and state-run rules on porn, few would advocate removing the ban on hardcore stuff on TV. There is a really interesting debate to be had here about speed limits, too. Is that personal liberty or reckless endangerment of other people's lives? How about if it's only in one specific lane of the motorway? Sorry. I'm getting carried away by liberal moral discussions. Back to 'free from' and 'free to'.

Freedom to do something is more focused on the equality side of liberalism. It's all very well to say that everyone is free to do what they want – start a business, work your way up a large company, whatever – but isn't all that much easier if you've had a leg-up with your start in life? If you were born to rich parents, you probably have the money, connections and the public-school education that make it an awful lot easier to start that business or climb that greasy pole.

What about people who are born poor, with a family history of unemployment? In a world without rules, where we are all free from all that government interference, how can they compete against the rest of the world? The world of casual labour and zero-hours contracts awaits. In that situation, are you free at all? Surely it's the bosses and the companies that are free to treat you as they wish?

Liberals who believe in 'freedom to' argue that the state needs to support people. That starts with an excellent education and lifelong healthcare to get people back on their feet – and back to work. And workers' rights that will protect individuals and their pursuit of happiness from the evils of big corporations.

These two camps of liberals can disagree quite strongly. At this point we need to talk about tax. Stay with me on this. One way that classical liberals (the ones who are all about 'freedom from') want us to be free is to be able to spend our money however we want. Freedom from tax. It's my money and those cat memes aren't going to buy themselves. These people aren't against all tax entirely. There is consensus from all the ideologies we'll be looking at in this book that some tax is inevitable. We all want schools and hospitals and all that. But for 'freedom from' liberals, tax should be at a minimum possible level.

So, there is no way that things like going to university – a free choice made by individuals in their own pursuit of happiness – should be paid for with taxpayers' money. To be clear here, by taxpayers we are talking about people who choose not to go to university as well as those who do. Which groups are least likely to go? Those with the least money. Things are changing in this respect, but if the government wants to subsidise university education, that basically means poor people paying for middle-class kids to get an extra advantage over them. Or so the argument goes.

Those liberals in the 'freedom to' camp, however, are big fans of the government levelling the playing field. That means, for example, making sure that university is a place that anyone can attend. If students are charged or saddled with massive amounts of debt, that makes it a privilege. No, extra money must be spent on university so there is equal opportunity and everyone is 'free to' do whatever they want.

These 'freedom to' liberals, then, are quite keen on government spending, which means that they have to be keen on tax. The money for public services has to come from somewhere. It's just another way that these two camps of liberals disagree.

Judging by the name, you might think that the Liberal Democrats are the home of British liberals and to some extent you might be right. Almost everyone within the Lib Dems would describe themselves as liberals. That said, there are many, many people in other parties who would also describe themselves as liberals. There are plenty in Labour, loads in the Conservative Party and even a good number in UKIP. This wide spread across the parties is partly down to the huge range of opinion within the liberal ideology.

In fact, in 1992 a man called Francis Fukuyama published a book called *The End of History and the Last Man*. He wasn't saying there would be no more events, but rather that liberal democracy is the globally victorious ideology. Everyone describes themselves and behaves as a liberal in some way. That's what we see in political parties in the UK. Everyone wants people to be free to behave as they wish, within the rules.

In 2019, we see that perhaps Fukuyama was a little premature in his description of the end of history. Both socialism (which believes in some level of instruction as opposed to pure liberty) and conservatism (which believes in hierarchy and roles for different people) have seen a distinct comeback.

While other parties all stand for at least some liberal policies, the Liberal Democrats have, over the years, provided us with the purest form. Indeed, a brief look at Liberal Democrat policies from the past fifteen years or so demonstrates the broad liberal church. Under Charles Kennedy, the party's 2005 manifesto had some standout liberal policies. See if you can spot which camp he was in. He wanted to scrap tuition fees; to introduce free personal care for elderly and disabled people; smaller class sizes in primary schools; to scrap Labour's plans of introducing ID cards.

Did you get it? Well done you. Have a biscuit. His Liberal Democrats were all about 'freedom to'. They were happy to spend a little more money in order to give people more opportunities and the best start in life. They believed that the state had a role to play in people's lives.

That position didn't last for long. Before the 2005 manifesto, a few Liberal Democrats had released *The Orange Book: Reclaiming Liberalism*, written by some people whose names you might recognise: Nick Clegg, Vince Cable, Ed Davey and David Laws, among others. The book was about the wonders of the free market, and how competition was the goal for our times. It would drive down cost and allow much more personal freedom.

If you recognised any of the names, you'll know that it's those liberals who took over the party in 2007. The next manifesto, in 2010, had four statements on the front cover: fair taxes that put money back in your pocket; a fair chance for every child; a fair future, creating jobs by making Britain greener; a fair deal, by cleaning up politics. Yes. They led with lower tax. Sure, a fair chance for children is in there too. Absolutely. But it's number two to tax cuts. That 'freedom from' is creeping into view.

The 2010 election ended up with the Liberal Democrats entering into a coalition government with the Conservative Party. We'll discuss conservatism in a minute but, like I say, many Conservatives consider themselves to be liberals. The Conservative form of liberalism, though, tends to be much more 'free from', as the Liberal Democrats became. Their new commitment to free-market liberal economics really allowed that match to happen.

As we've seen, all liberals are fans of freedom, in some form or another. But some are absolute fanatics. We call them libertarians.

Libertarians

When you go to watch a football match, there is always one stand that sings and chants its way through the game with a little more oomph than the rest. At Chelsea it's the Matthew

Harding Stand. At Liverpool it's the Kop. At Arsenal it's . . . oh, hang on, nobody sings at Arsenal. In Europe they call their super fans the Ultras. These are the people for whom the club is more than a hobby. It's everything for them. They live, eat and sleep their chosen club.

And so it is with liberals. Everyone here believes in freedom and (to some extent) equality, but while the rest of you are enjoying your little sing-song, there is a corner of the ground that's going wild. The Liberal Ultras. The libertarians.

Libertarians believe that any state involvement in their lives takes away their freedom. The state should, therefore, be the smallest it possibly can be – economically and otherwise. This means absolute minimum government spending, taxation and policing – and no CCTV checking up on what you're doing all the time.

Some of their views can feel quite extreme, too. In mainstream politics, most people tend to be fans of the green belt – that nice bit of leafy land surrounding big cities. People generally argue that it operates as the lungs for the city and keeps things nicer for everyone. Not libertarians, though. They might argue that keeping the land free from development drives up house prices inside that belt. Much like that bottle of coke from the only vendor at the train station, if there are limited options for the house buyer, house prices go up. Not only that, but it might also drive developers to build on green spaces inside the city in an attempt to squeeze as much housing out of the area as possible.

28

There are quite a few libertarians in UK politics. For a while UKIP positioned itself as a libertarian party. Within the Conservative Party there are libertarians, too. David Davis, the former Brexit minister, describes himself as a libertarian. He has criticised the public for not defending our freedom enough. Speaking to the *Guardian* in 2015, he said we had 'idly let [extra surveillance] happen'.

There are many more libertarians in America. The whole 'Tea Party' movement in the Republican Party from a few years ago was fully libertarian. People in this camp see government intervention as the absolute enemy. They also tend to be more extreme than their UK counterparts. The Libertarian Party stand on a platform of abolishing the welfare state and the state-school system, a fully free-market-based healthcare system and more. When it comes to personal freedom they are equally clear. Abortion? Up to the individual. Capital punishment? Absolutely not. LGBTQ+ issues? Up to the individual – nothing to do with the state.

This is the extreme end of liberalism. But as we've seen, there are plenty of people who would describe themselves as liberals across the political spectrum, including in the Conservative Party.

Conservatism

First off, conservatism and the Conservative Party are not the same thing. This is a little confusing. Sure, some Conservatives are conservatives. But not all of them. And even though some of them are, they can still disagree about what being a conservative is, even if they can shake hands on what being a Conservative is. Clear? Excellent.

If liberals like freedom, what conservatives put at the top of their list is tradition. Not necessarily because they are massive fans of the eighteenth century (although some of them are), but because they are massive fans of where we are today. Conservatives look around at everything we've achieved, the progress we've made, the wonderful institutions of the country, and say, 'Yeah, this is pretty great.'

If you've established that we are in a good place – not perfect, nobody thinks anywhere is perfect – then you have to ask how we got here. What was it about everything that has happened before that has led us to be where we are right now? The answer to that, my friends, is our British traditions and customs. Our way of doing things.

It comes down to this: the status quo works. Not only because it got us to where we are, but also because we all feel a sense of belonging. We can all feel that we are part of this. This is our country and we love it.

At the Conservative Party Conference in October 2018, Jeremy Hunt, then foreign secretary, said: 'Remember in our Great British history the right thing has often happened – but it never happens by accident. It happens when brave people take smart decisions . . . when our talents come together . . . and when we draw on the strengths of our past to chart a route to the future. The essence of Conservatism.'

All these wonderful things that we've done in the past have shaped where we are today. But Conservatives are clear that we don't want to stick with every aspect of the past. There is no suggestion that we return to Oliver Twist's workhouse system, or that we revive slavery. No, the traditions that we need to continue and to build on are the 'strengths of our past'.

What exactly are the 'strengths of our past'? Hunt didn't elaborate on that, but it's interesting to look back at something Theresa May said during the 2017 general election. She was on *The One Show* with her husband and she said that, around the house, 'there's boy jobs and girl jobs'. This might sound like a pretty remarkable statement for the second female prime minister of the country to make. But when people disagreed with her comment (and as this was made during an election campaign, I'm sure you can imagine that there were one or two people queuing up to suggest that this wasn't a brilliant thing for her to say), they were imagining that the 'girl jobs' are in some way *less* than the 'boy jobs'. Or even if they're not *less*, they are still different and rely on some kind of outdated stereotypes. But conservatives don't necessarily see it that way.

Conservatives believe in taking the best from the past – and that can include the traditional breakdown of household chores. It doesn't demean someone to do the tasks that their mother and grandmother did. Far from it, taking on the jobs and skills that have been handed down over the years and the generations can feel comforting, even satisfying. As though you're part of something.

It might be seen as a conservative tradition that one person (normally the woman) stays at home with the children.

It's not demeaning, it's working as a family unit. Sure, officially the person going to work gets paid while the other doesn't, but that money is going into the family – not to the wage earner. Each person in this family unit has their demarked role. Each person in the family is valued. This is taking 'the strengths of our past to chart a route to the future'.

These family units, built around tradition and trust and love, are the perfect building blocks for communities. Along with the idea of private property and home ownership, your family gives you a stake in the game. It means that what happens to you, to your neighbours, to your community, matters. You have a corner of the world that you care deeply about. You want it to succeed, so you work harder to make sure you've played your part in making that happen. Neighbourhood watch schemes, litter picking, street parties, summer fetes, Christmas drinks, all these things begin to emerge and bring communities together.

Jobs are also better mapped out for different people, because some are naturally better than others at them and people should really do the roles that have been defined for them. Women might be better carers or prime ministers, or whatever. Men might make better construction workers, charity bosses or city bankers. Or other jobs that don't begin with 'c'.

It's not just about some Calvinist-style system of predetermination. Conservatives also believe in a meritocracy: the best will rise to the top. They can lead the rest through it all.

That's 'our talents coming together'. That's the conservative dream. Sure, it is likely that you'll vaguely conform to the kind of job that your parents did. But there is also scope for promotion and seniority. In a meritocracy you can rise to the top of an organisation, but you have to work for it.

A quick look at the Conservative MPs elected in 2017 shows us this: 45 per cent of them went to private school. Within that, nearly 7 per cent of them went to Eton. That's from a pool of just 7 per cent of the country going to any private school. So we see that meritocracy is possible, but traditional demarked roles still have their place.

Take, for example, the concept of grammar schools. All children take a test at the age of eleven and their secondary school is determined by the outcome of that test. Do really well and you're off to grammar school, where your academic talent can be nurtured. Don't do quite so well? Not a problem, it's off to secondary modern for you, where you can have an education that's more suited to you. Society is being formed on its merits.

Like that Young Fathers album you bought on CD when they won the Mercury Music Award, but you now use as a coaster, meritocracy is useful in more ways than one. Actually, not really like that album, because that's only ever going to be a coaster now. As well as ensuring the people best suited for the job will be running things, meritocracy also encourages those people to reach their full potential. If you believe that hard work leads to the opportunity to succeed, you will be motivated to work hard. But if the system looks rigged, you just won't bother. This is also one of the reasons conservatives like the free market. The free market reflects the value of whatever role you end up doing, and that chimes with this idea of people rising to the top because of their natural abilities.

You may be reading this and saying, 'Hang on – conservatism backs suitable roles for people *and* meritocracy, tradition *and* the free market?'. If you were thinking that, well spotted! That's why conservatism can be so nebulous. To understand it we have to go back to the idea of taking what's good from our past and helping it shape our present. The Bank of England (and the City of London as a whole) is a British institution. If you are clever enough, maybe you can escape the work your parents did and end up working there. And people are encouraged to chase that dream. It's interesting to note that the slogan for the Conservative Party Conference in 2018 was a single word: opportunity.

So, conservatism believes very strongly that we are all different. And that some of us are better than others, which leads to a natural hierarchy. And, most importantly, that's OK.

At the top of the hierarchy in the UK we've got the Queen. This shows how varied conservatism can be. American conservatives – the Republicans – are passionate about not having a monarchy. Their name literally means people who don't want to be burdened by a king or queen. Conservatives in the UK, though, are really, really keen on the monarchy. They think it is a wonderful institution, full of history and significance, as well as a force for good in the world, helping to give the nation stability, shape and character. And let's be clear here, stability is the name of the game. Stability of community, of the markets, and of politics. That's in stark contrast to socialism or, more specifically, Marxism, which preaches revolution and sweeping change.

Another useful aspect of Her Majesty is that she provides a form of authority. Not directly, of course. If you share a drunken kiss with someone you shouldn't, you're not going to have our reigning monarch stop by your house and tell you off. Unless that person was, say, Prince Charles. Even then, probably not. And you're probably not that likely to be smooching with him anyway. You strike me as more of a Harry person.

Authority is very important for conservatives. That's because they believe that we're all pretty flawed. We're imperfect, jealous, greedy, needy. Left to our own devices, we'll stray considerably far from the ideal of the community, with its Sunday afternoon get-togethers. That's why, as we discussed, things like tradition, property, opportunity and even family are so important – they give you a reason to work hard. A reason to give a shit. But sometimes that carrot of community will only get you so far. So authority is needed too, and that can come from a wide range of places.

You won't be surprised to hear that conservatives are quite big on the church – specifically the Church of England, but any church will do. It creates all kinds of community vibes and it provides routine and structure on your

Sunday. These are Good Things. It also establishes a degree of authority: there are rules and you are reminded to follow them.

Not everyone goes to church, though, so there have to be other forms of authority as well. The family chips in here too. Families have rules and order and structure to them, a sense of moral authority. If you've been out illicitly smooching again, you may face some fairly stern disapproval from your family. It's not against the law, but it's definitely the Wrong Thing.

The police and the courts are the final word on authority. Ultimately, if you break the law of the land, you're going to be in trouble. The rule of law is vital to keep people in check. The police should be a friendly face in the community, because everyone should be doing the Right Thing anyway. But their presence is there as a reminder, a deterrent. A six-year-old told me once at a workshop that the police are there to help you if you need them and to stop bad people. That's exactly how conservatives see it.

For all that, there are actually very few people who identify themselves as pure conservatives today. Much, much more common is the concept of one-nation conservatism.

One-nation conservatism

This is a variety of conservatism that dates back to Conservative Prime Minister Benjamin Disraeli in the nineteenth century. Recognising the economic split in the country that had been caused by the Industrial Revolution, he said it looked like two different nations. His idea was that in an organic society everyone should look out for each other, and that the wealthy had a responsibility to support those in need.

In short, he wanted rich people to cough up to pay for stuff. He used the fancy term *noblesse oblige* which pretty much means noble people are obliged to do things for the good of society. To provide services that people need, such as education, health and benefits.

Things have changed quite a lot since then. Back then the Old Etonians, the Royal Engineers and Oxford University used to dominate the FA Cup. And there was no internet. See? Very different. Today's one-nation conservatives, though, still believe that we need to look after those who have been dealt a hand of cards that just isn't so great.

When Theresa May, a self-identified one-nation conservative, took over as prime minister in 2016, she made a speech on the steps of Downing Street that had some very conservative themes. When she said, 'We will do everything we can to help anybody, whatever your background, to go as far as your talents will take you', she was talking about meritocracy, that natural hierarchy that conservatives believe in so much.

The speech wasn't just conservative, though. She didn't mention the words 'tradition' or 'past' even once. Instead she spoke almost entirely about the 'burning injustices' facing the country. She could have been talking exactly about the two nations that Disraeli spoke of all those years ago when she said:

'If you're born poor, you will die on average nine years earlier than others. If you're black, you're treated more harshly by the criminal justice system than if you're white. If you're a white, working-class boy, you're less likely than anybody else in Britain to go to university. If you're at a state school, you're less likely to reach the top professions than if you're educated privately.'

These are all instances in which the rich, white privileged members of society (and let's face it, that includes many, many members of her own party) have a different, easier life. Maybe they really do inhabit that second, parallel nation. A nation with private healthcare, private education and private security. But Theresa May was saying she wanted to unite those countries again by increasing the opportunities for those who aren't part of the privileged nation.

She ended the speech by combining that idea with a sense of patriotism and confidence born out of past success:

'And I know because we're Great Britain, that we will rise to the challenge. As we leave the European Union, we will forge a bold new positive role for ourselves in the world, and we will make Britain a country that works not for a privileged few, but for every one of us.

'That will be the mission of the government I lead, and together we will build a better Britain.'

Theresa May was talking about change on a scale that your regular conservative wouldn't be a huge fan of. We can see one-nation conservatism is an ideology that is prepared to break away from its roots in order to bring people together in that 'one nation'.

Socialism

What socialists really value is equality. That's the thing they put front and centre. Everything else has to come after that. We're all people, we're all born equal, we should all be equal.

Ah ha! I hear you say. Equality. That's what liberals want too, isn't it? Those French revolutionaries, they wanted 'Liberté, Égalité, Fraternité'. The American Declaration of Independence was all about 'all men are created equal' as well. Equality is definitely a liberal ideal.

Yes, in a way. But Socialists look around at this liberal world and see a rigged system. The whole idea of freedom and equality is nonsense. The notion that we can all be equally free to do what we want is a myth. For most people, the cards are stacked against them and this is the only game in town.

Do you remember all that stuff about the free market? How wonderful it is to be able to act in our own self interests, make our own choices. How happy it makes liberals, and conservatives, for that matter? Well . . . socialists don't really agree. They hate the free market. A lot. My advice? Don't bring it up in conversation with a socialist. It won't end well.

They look at the free market and they cry 'Foul!' They point to the fact that if you happen to be particularly good at, say, banking, you will be paid inordinate amounts of money for your skills. If you're good at something else, let's say caring for other people, then you will be paid incredibly little for your time. It's not fair and it's not right.

If you do go into detail with them about the whole thing (I can't stress enough how bad an idea that is), a lot of their anger is saved for the profit motive.

They say that the free market encourages people to get stuck in so that they can earn more money. That's their only motivation. Sure, the argument goes that we can somehow also make everyone else happy while in pursuit of our own happiness. But that's clearly nonsense, because all people want is profit. Not the happiness and welfare of our fellow humans. Not the eradication of prejudice and injustice. Oh no. It's all about money.

How can a system be good if everyone is trying to squeeze as much money out of everyone else as possible? That's literally how supply and demand works, figuring out the highest price most people are willing to pay for what you're selling.

The profit motive requires us to put money and financial gain above caring for and helping other people. It means that we spend our time working out how to make our businesses more efficient to make more money, which might ultimately lead to firing as many people as possible. Yeah, they don't have a job any more, but it means I'm a bit richer. Whoop. Go me.

The basis of the capitalist system isn't just the free market, it's 'capital': the resources that you need to do something. Most often, that's money. And this is where socialists see the system as being particularly unfair. People who are born with money are able to operate in a way that people who aren't born with money can't. Their lives are easier from day one.

If you don't need to earn money, you can focus on your studies. You can afford to go to university – and not have to support yourself with a job when you're there. You can take on unpaid internships. You can use some kind of old-boys network to ensure that you get a well-paid job. So, there you are. Born rich, now earning lots of money and getting richer. Your children? They're going to be born rich, too. The pattern continues.

Most people, though, have to work from a young age and they need to work hard, because when you're on the minimum wage you need to put in a lot of hours to pay the bills. A-levels, perhaps even GCSEs, are taken while balancing studies with part-time work. Results suffer. Sure, in theory you have the freedom to choose whether or not to go to university, but perhaps the financial burden is just too much. Fine, you still have the freedom to choose your job, but without a degree, or with poorer results, there aren't as many opportunities. It comes down to a choice of minimum-wage jobs, possibly on zero-hour contracts. Now you're free to spend your money however you like. But perhaps it doesn't feel very free when you have to spend 50 per cent of your wages on rent – before you even think about food and bills.

In short, according to socialists, the great education system that is supposed to ensure we're all given an equal start in life is rigged to make the rich richer and to keep the workers in their place. Let's not forget that the rich need workers to make their lifestyle possible. It's the workers who make stuff in the factories, or the cafes, or the 'fulfilment centres'.

The system, socialists believe, just doesn't work for most people. It's not designed to. When Jeremy Corbyn launched his 2017 general election campaign, he called it 'a rigged system set up by the wealth extractors, for the wealth extractors'.

Socialists have an alternative vision. And it is radically different. They don't want to touch up the paintwork of the current system, they want to bring it crashing down. This is not a liberal ideology – as we've seen, they think this whole freedom thing is a myth. To tear down those walls, individual liberty needs to be limited. People can't just do what they want and to hell with everyone else. That's the old way. We need a big government to ensure the smooth working of . . . well, everything. They want to achieve real equality, making sure that everyone is provided for and that everyone is chipping in as best they can. The idea is, to use a phrase that Karl Marx made popular, 'From each according to his ability, to each according to his needs'. That means you are expected to work as hard as you can, just as you do today.

You still need to work at the place best suited to your skills, whether that's teaching or farming or playing Iago in a regionally touring theatre group. But the good news is that you'll be working for your community. Your country. Everything you make contributes in some way to the future. Even if you're doing the same job, it's so much more satisfying than working for The Man. Nobody likes the thought of working hard to make, say, Richard Branson or Jeff Bezos richer. That's no ·

42

fun. But to do it to make your community richer? To create a better world for your family? That's worth working for.

At the same time, everyone gets a more equal share in return, no matter what your role is. There is no arbitrary valuation of your job. Your hard work as a cleaner is just as valuable as someone else's hard work in the office in which you have cleaned. So, pay awards aren't about the profitability of your role. Remember how awful the profit motive is? Well, that. We don't do things to squeeze more money from other people any more. That was the old way.

We are now 'paid' according to what we need. That means everyone has housing and food and heating. That doesn't sound like all that much, but in the liberal world we live in right now, thousands are stuck with the choice of eating or heating. Not if everyone was supplied 'to each according to their needs'. The elderly and the disabled would be given more, because they need more, regardless of their contribution.

You'll notice, therefore, that often the most able bodied and gifted people might be required to work the hardest and may receive the least. They have the highest 'abilities' and lowest 'needs'. If you're reading this and thinking, 'Sucks to be them, right?', socialism isn't for you. You're too stuck in the old, rigged system, thinking of people as individuals. That's not how socialists see us. We're a collective. It's through divisive individualistic messaging that the system has kept us down for so long, when in fact we could all benefit much more if we worked together as a community.

Speaking at the Labour Party Conference in 2018, John McDonnell said, 'One hundred years ago in 1918 the Labour Party adopted Clause Four as part of our party's constitution. Let me remind you what it said: "to secure for the workers, by hand or by brain, the full fruits of their industry." I say the Clause 4 principles are as relevant today as they were back then. Fair, democratic, collective solutions to the challenges of the modern economy.'

Note the word 'fair' at the start of his list. Socialists still love equality as much as they ever have. To achieve that fairness, socialism is about community and cooperation. This means that, rather than everything being owned privately – and in competition with everything else – socialists want common ownership. Everything from land to banks to industry should be collectively owned by the people and used for the people. The profit motive becomes history.

The trouble is, not all socialists agree on the path to achieving this utopia. Karl Marx was a revolutionary socialist. He believed that the rich and powerful will never give up their wealth and control – and that the only way to get them to do so is for the masses to rise up against them. He thought that it was only through a bloody battle that this new world – a world in which the worker was valued and powerful – could be forged.

Others disagreed. Members of the Fabian Society, established soon after Marx's death in the late nineteenth century, said that revolution was unnecessary. Instead what was needed was for working people to be given the vote. Surely, they argued, working people would only ever vote for a party that promised to put them first, giving them the equality they deserve. In short, working people would only vote for socialist parties. The group went on to become one of the founding organisations of the Labour Party.

It's worth recognising here a group of organisations that helped to form the Labour Party and have been instrumental within the party ever since: the trade unions. Workers coming together to demand better pay and conditions in their industry. Trade unions have campaigned on socialist values for their entire existence. Since the late nineteenth century, many union members have supported the Labour Party both financially and in the ballot box.

Of course workers getting the vote (in 1918, since you asked) did not immediately transform the UK into a socialist state, but it's this form of gradual evolution that is generally favoured by British socialists today – especially those inside the Labour Party.

The Labour Party has been many, many things over the years. I'm not going to go back and give a running commentary over ideological pasts during which, say, Hugh Gaitskell handed over the party to George Brown and Harold Wilson. No. That would be for someone much, much wiser than me to do.

We are, though, going to look at the concept of social democracy. That's because it's at the heart of a very important ideological battle in the Labour Party right now.

Social democracy

The most recent Labour government, under Tony Blair and, subsequently, Gordon Brown, wasn't a socialist government. It was a social democratic government. Social democrats believe that equality can be realised through the power of the free market. It's a lot like a really strong Fabian Society approach – we're not going to have a revolution, we're just going to change the rules a little to make the game work in our favour.

That might seem a little odd if you remember that socialists hate the free market. Here we have people who claim to be on the socialist side of the fence, preaching all about equality, and yet they are also saying that the free market is their friend, that banking is a vital part of the system, and that they can legislate to stave off the worst parts of capitalism.

Social democrats get the idea that capitalism, like Simon Cowell, can be a bit horrible, exploiting workers and creating winners and losers. People need to be protected, so, like Ant and Dec putting their arms around vulnerable young singers, in 1998 the Labour government introduced the Human Rights Act and the Minimum Wage Act.

With people protected from the worst things that the free market can do to them (in theory, at least), the social democratic government could turn to harnessing the sweet, sweet efficiency of the system. A scheme called private finance initiative (PFI) was introduced. This was supposed to get private companies to invest their own money into public services. We, the people, would get sparkling new schools and hospitals;

private companies would get a long-term return on their investments. Nobody would be exploited. The birds would sing just a little bit louder. Everything would be pretty great.

Clearly socialists hate the idea of any form of privatisation. They think that the profit motive and healthcare, for example, just don't mix. Social democrats, though, don't think it's the end of the world. Why not use some free-market efficiency to improve our healthcare system? Right now, some of those PFI deals aren't looking quite as amazing as they once did (it turns out that companies weren't fooled into making the investments, and they were allowed to trap public services into huge repayments). But that's not really the point of this section. We're looking at the ideology, not how it's panned out in practice.

Another interesting example is education. There is evidence that the attainment gap between wealthy and poor children starts very early in life. Children might arrive at primary school with a huge difference in prior learning. Research from Teach First has shown that 'poorer children in every part of the country are more likely to start school behind their better-off peers.' That's not what equality looks like.

Socialists might use this as clear evidence that we need to rip up the whole system and transform the world, but social democrats aren't so radical in their solutions. Instead, the Blair government introduced Sure Start centres, specifically designed to work with 'poorer children' who might otherwise end up being behind when they start school. It's not a massive change, but the theory was that it would be enough. The children and parents just needed a leg-up. This wasn't about withdrawing freedom and forcing people to take parenting classes, or raise their children in specific ways. No, this was about incentivising and supporting struggling parents.

So, there we go. The social democrats tried a number of initiatives like this when they had their time in government, but now the socialists are in charge of the Labour Party. Those who still believe in social democracy are referred to as Blairites and even 'red Tories'. But despite the differences between them, social democrats do agree with socialists that equality is fundamental. They just disagree very strongly on how to achieve it.

Similarities

Now we've had a look at these ideologies, as well as some of their offshoots, let's just stop for a minute to see what we can pick out.

While there can be crossover between them, liberalism, conservatism and socialism are generally pretty far apart. The contrasting focuses on freedom, tradition and equality mean they should blend like a Little Mix fan at a Slayer concert. Assimilation is tricky.

And yet and yet and yet. We live in a world of Spotify. The album appears to be getting lost.

Everyone listens to a little of everything these days. There is a real possibility that someone might like a bit of Little

Mix interspersed with the seminal album *Reign In Blood*. For many, the old rules of commitment to a single genre are over.

In much the same way, there are very few classical liberals or straight-out conservatives in mainstream British politics today. Like Turkey Twizzlers, these relatively extreme perspectives are harder to find these days. (If I was writing this a few years ago, I would have included socialists in this, but it's quite clear that there are plenty of socialists in mainstream British politics.)

What are we left with? Progressive liberals, one-nation conservatives and social democrats. What is really interesting is how similar the end results of those ideologies are. They may come from very different starting points, but they come together to agree on a whole lot of stuff.

Let's go back to that speech that Theresa May gave when she became prime minister. That one about the 'burning injustices'. Here's another extract: 'If you're a woman, you will earn less than a man. If you suffer from mental health problems, there's not enough help to hand. If you're young, you'll find it harder than ever before to own your own home.'

That first line, about women earning less than men? That's about equality and, to a certain extent, it's about freedom – but that progressive freedom, 'freedom to', not 'freedom from'. It's something that one-nation conservatives, progressive liberals and social democrats can all get behind. As for helping people with mental health problems? That couldn't be more 'freedom to'! It's also 'to each according to their needs'. This was a newly appointed Conservative prime minister making promises that people from across the mainstream political spectrum could get behind.

For further proof of the similarities, let's have a look at some of the recent slogans from the main parties. The Conservative slogan was: 'A country that works for everyone'. Labour went with: 'For the many not the few'. The Liberal Democrats wanted a 'Stronger economy. Fairer Society. Opportunity for Everyone.'

Given that, under Jeremy Corbyn, Labour now self-identifies as a socialist party, I find it amazing that all the parties promise almost exactly the same thing.

These ideologies come together on a number of practical policies, trying to hit the key public concerns. The NHS is something that many, many people care deeply about. At the 2017 election, therefore, everyone promised to raise extra money for the service. The promises of funding were generally very similar. Of course, they have ideologically different standpoints on health – not least through the involvement of private companies – but on a grand scale they all want more money to fund a better, free-at-the-point-of-use health service.

There's a boyband vibe at work here. They all play up the differences: the sporty one, the cute one, the one who wants to stop selling arms to Saudi Arabia. In reality, though, there is at least some consensus on what the problems are among one-nation conservatives, progressive liberals and social democrats.

I'm not saying that the parties are identical. They aren't. They still have different ideologies and solutions to the problems they see. Let's look at that last line in the extract from May's speech.

She made a point about women's equality and mental health. Everyone is on board there. So far in the speech she had already spoken about the barriers to working-class white kids and about police treatment of black people. If only they had trusted her a bit more (and if only people actually watched these things), heads would have been nodding wildly in front of televisions across the country.

And then, in the midst of these big topics, as if it is an equal issue, she talks about how young people may never be able to own their home. Now that's pure conservatism. Owning property, owning anything, is massive for Team Conservative. They think that it helps you get involved with your community. They are frantically waving the flag for home ownership. Remember how Thatcher made it possible for people to buy their own council house? That.

Now, the others? Not so much. Good quality housing for all? Absolutely. Everyone having good enough housing, at a reasonable cost, to pursue their personal vision of happiness? Bang on. Owning a house? Not so much.

Likewise, the various parties might agree that something is a problem but disagree on the solution. Everyone, for example, thinks that rough sleeping is pretty bad. Sure, it's gone up since 2010, but the Conservative Party is aware of it and is (at the time of writing) trying to do something. The right thing? Who knows. People come up with all sorts of solutions to the problems we see. You don't have to watch politics very long to see that there is a huge range of opinion on almost everything. Politicians tackle the huge questions of how our daily lives should be led from very different angles, with the inevitable difference of opinion that comes with that.

This is the point. These more moderate versions of the traditional ideologies are similar, but they do still nod back to their roots.

The way politicians present their beliefs is often pragmatic, as well – it can shift in order to fit the narrative of the time. Right now, it's important to demonstrate a commitment to fighting for 'everyone' or 'the many'. The idea that for far too long, politics has just been about the elite has won out. David Cameron, Hillary Clinton and others discovered very publicly that being from 'the establishment' (Cameron went to Eton and Oxford, Clinton had been First Lady for eight years) does you no favours. No, you need to prove your credentials as a politician of the people. Standing up for 'the regular folk' works. So that's what everyone does.

The breakdown of trust

Throughout these populist messages, one of the main reasons all the main parties are so keen on describing themselves as being for 'everyone' is because of the assumption that politicians *aren't* in it for everyone. They're in it for themselves and/or for big businesses to make money from you and me. In short, the public think that politicians are working for a very small section of society.

As you can imagine, I talk about politics a lot. To anyone who will stand near me for long enough to get going. I hear a lot of these complaints, things like: 'They're all the same', 'They're all just in it for themselves', 'They aren't really in charge, it's all some other group/individual pulling the strings'. Often accompanied by lots of swearing and rather violent imagery. It seems as though a lot of the public have a pretty poor opinion of most politicians. So I want to take a moment to explain why I trust MPs. Why I think they're (mostly) good people.

'They're all in it for themselves' is the one I hear most often, to be honest. This idea that every decision MPs (and councillors for that matter) make is based around some kind of selfish agenda. To look at what is actually going on, it might make sense to look back at how people get involved in politics in the first place. How a politician is 'born'. The moment of engagement is fairly nebulous. It might come about through a growing awareness of the many problems our country faces, or it can get kickstarted by a single issue. I first became interested in politics through animal rights – as a teenager the injustices inflicted upon innocent animals in the name of scientific, culinary, sporting or fashion delights blew my mind. That was what did it for me, but everyone is different. The war in Iraq incited plenty of people. More recently Grenfell directed a lot of attention towards politics. Brexit. Gun laws in America. Even anger about having to put our clocks forward and back every year.

However you become engaged, once you've taken an

interest you may well find your way to a political party that best represents your life view, your ideology, your vision for the future. Maybe you've taken some kind of online quiz – the wonderful Vote for Policies is always a nice start. You hit Google (or your trendy search alternative) and find out when and where your local party meets.

Depending on how fired up you are and how much time you have, you may then find yourself attending small meetings in cold, cramped spaces. Wandering the streets on dark, damp evenings putting your leaflets through the doors of people who, probably, won't read them. This stuff is boring, physically uncomfortable and can feel incredibly thankless. But you do it anyway. Because you believe that the party you're supporting really needs to win; it's the only one that can make the changes that are needed. That other lot? They're going to ruin the country. You'll do whatever you can.

If you are particularly committed, you may be asked to consider putting yourself forward for a local council seat. Quite probably one that you have no hope of winning. Most seats don't change hands very often. So you put in a bit more work. Those Tuesdays out leafleting become *every* evening. And weekend. Your partner isn't delighted. Neither are your kids, for that matter. They'd quite like you to come home occasionally. You're talking to people, shaking hands and, yes, even kissing babies. If this is what you have to do for a chance of being on that council and improving your area and your community, then so be it.

You lose that election. You were always going to. You knew that. But then, campaigning felt quite hopeful, you spoke to lots of people who said they'd vote for you. So you enter the fight to be selected as your party's candidate.

Just typing this, I feel mean for keeping you out of office for so long, so I'm going to give you this one. After years of hard campaigning, you've made it onto the council. Don't forget that many of your activist colleagues will never even get this far. There are very few Green Party councillors, but they have lots of activists. They are happy fighting from the bottom up their entire life.

You're a councillor for a while, you still do the evening leafletting, but you also go to council meetings and committee meetings and so on. Your pay is almost zero. But you can start to make a difference in your area. Or at least you can do your best to stop the party that's in power locally from messing it all up.

At some point – normally after years on the council – the opportunity to run for your party in a general election might come up. Remember, these are normally every five years. That's a long time if you don't quite make the selection on the first attempt. And, again, there is no guarantee of a win. Or, if there is a very good chance your party will win, there is a *much* harder battle to be selected. You'll probably need many more years on the council first.

With the wind in your sails, let's say that years later you do make it. You run in a general election. You win. You're an MP. Take a bow. What is it that kept you going all those years? The fantasy that one day you could maybe fiddle an expenses system and get a free bedside table? That you'll finally get the chance to slide your hand over a researcher's taut, bronzed arm? Or the opportunity to align yourself with some shady group or individual who holds all the real power, effectively throwing away your chance at wielding any influence, after all that effort?

Do you know what? I'm saying no to that. I'm saying that the vast majority of MPs have been down that road, and after that long, monotonous slog, they really do want to make the country better.

Another complaint some people have is that once they are in a position of influence, MPs are only interested in making themselves rich – and screw the people, who cares about the people? They point, for example, to some MPs and members of the House of Lords who own shares in private healthcare providers and vote to increase the use of the free market within the NHS, something that may well make them better off.

Voting for a policy that might make you richer does, I'll readily admit, look a little, well, dodgy. But let's give them the benefit of the doubt for a moment; perhaps they're not voting for something because it benefits them personally, but because that policy is firmly in line with their ideology. Let's have a look at it in a different way.

Instead of the NHS – a notoriously contentious area, as we'll see later – let's imagine a Green Party MP supporting a policy of renewable energy. Perhaps they have a bit of spare money, they might decide that they want to invest in windfarms. They look at the financial benefits – we need more renewable energy and we live on a pretty windy island, so it's likely to be a good investment. They also want to support the windfarm industry. They want their money to make the world a better place. They've found a way to make an investment work for them and for the whole country.

When there is a great big debate in the Commons, this Green MP is going to vote for windfarms, right? Because they really, really like windfarms. They dream of windfarms. Their wallpaper has a windfarm pattern on it. Their children are called 'Turbine' and 'Renew'. So, yeah, darn straight they are going to vote for more windfarms every single time they get the opportunity.

So . . . is that corruption at work? Is this MP telling the world that it can go jump off a cliff – they're bringing home the bacon, baby? I don't think so. I think this is someone having principles – and it's those principles that got them elected in the first place. The people who voted for them probably knew about this windfarm love. They might even feel betrayed if this MP turned around and said that they were voting against windfarms on this occasion.

So, if that seems a reasonable position, let's look again briefly at the NHS. Now, let's imagine we've got an MP who really, really believes in the free market, in privatisation, in capitalism, really believes that this system has, over the past century, improved the lives of people all over the globe. Yes, that person is most likely to be found in the Conservative Party.

This Conservative MP really knows the benefits of privatisation and the free market. They think that the less regulation and the more competition, the better. It's very possible that they look at the NHS, at our aging population and cracking infrastructure, and they think about all the wonderful benefits of privatisation – investment, efficiencies, freedom from political interference. They have a vision of an NHS that works for everyone because of the help from that beautiful free market – and they want to make it happen.

They invest in the future that they want. It's good for their investment returns (like the windfarm was for the Green MP) and it's good for their vision of making the NHS great and sustainable. Everybody wins. Obviously, given their ideological passion for helping the NHS with some free market love, they are going to vote for more use of the free market in the NHS. Just like the Green MP who was elected by an electorate fully aware of their perspective on wind farms, the electorate presumably know how much their MP loves the free market. Their children are called 'Laissez' and 'Faire'. They are expected to vote the way they said they would.

OK. You might have read that and be thinking, 'What a load of nonsense'. And, yeah, there probably are some MPs you can think of who might be a little more, shall we say, self-serving, than others. Quite possibly they are the ones who didn't have to take that long and thankless journey to become an MP or a politician. They can't all be perfect.

The point of this book, though, is to help you make sense of this messed-up political landscape. It's OK to disagree with people – and just because you disagree with them doesn't make them evil. Once you accept that, it's possible to look at their actions and see them as positive steps towards their vision for the country.

Which is why I choose to trust MPs. Whether or not you agree with their ideologies or policies, I hope you do too.

And finally, a quick reminder . . .

You may have read through this section and found one way of thinking, one ideology, considerably more appealing than another. You may have dropped the book and shouted, 'Yes! Finally, someone said it!' That's fine. It's OK to have an ideology that you sign up to. But if you're going to try to make sense of this political landscape, you have to understand that it doesn't make you better than anyone else. Or more correct. You just disagree. And that's OK.

PART TWO

A Tour of the Battlegrounds

We now know where everyone starts from. Some believe in tradition while some want freedom. But it's all a bit theoretical. What does that mean in real life? How does that change your conversation down the pub? This is what we need to get in order to really make sense of the political landscape: to really understand how other people are driven.

In Part One, we looked at Christmas – but here's a much more concrete example of policy being shaped by ideology.

In 2017, *Blue Planet II* was on TV. Everyone watched it and decided that they didn't like plastic anymore. One easy way to cut back on plastic is plastic straws. People disagreed on how to deal with it, though, because . . . well, because of course they did. Here's where the different ideologies might stand:

Liberals and libertarians: Straws are wrong but we can trust in the free market to respond to the problem on its own. Look, in reaction to public opinion many cafes and restaurants have already stopped using them voluntarily. No new rules needed. We can maintain our liberty.

Socialists: Straws are wrong, they should be banned. Immediately. How can it be OK to keep using things we have decided are wrong? Sure, many cafes and restaurants have stopped, but have they all?

Traditional conservatives: We've been using straws for a long time. We should make more of an effort to recycle and dispose of them properly – that way they won't end up in the seas and oceans. But, really, it's not us causing the issue in the seas. China, Indonesia and the Philippines are the ones causing most of the damage. Cutting down our use of straws would make no difference.

One-nation conservatives/social democrats: Straws are wrong. They pollute and use too many natural resources to create. Relying on the free market might not be enough to stop their use entirely. But we can't ban them now because companies and livelihoods are based on the plastic-straw industry. We'll ban them in five to ten years' time, giving these companies the chance to prepare and reduce their reliance on straws.

So, there we have it – all those positions are reasonable. They all make sense. They can all be justified. If we are to leave our echo chambers we need to recognise that. Nobody is a demon if they believe in the free market or if they want to ban straws. (Obviously, there are exceptions. If you didn't enjoy *Blue Planet II*, or don't like David Attenborough, you're just wrong. And, probably, evil.)

If there is such a huge difference between perspectives on something as simple as plastic straws, imagine how it must be for the big issues of the day.

In this section, we'll take a walk through some of the biggest battlegrounds in British politics. These are the areas that politicians of all ideologies have fought over for decades. We've looked at how parties can sometimes follow their different paths to the same conclusions – that's not what this section is about. This is about those areas where everyone disagrees. Fundamentally.

If you're not a fan of conflict and argument, you may be tempted to give this bit a miss. Don't do that. This is at the very heart of making sense of this messed-up world. You have to be able to listen to someone making an argument with which you profoundly disagree and understand where they are coming from. They're not ignorant. They want the best for the country, just like you. They just see things differently.

What are we going to be looking at? Here's what: privatisation, tax and the welfare state, education, immigration, free speech, Brexit and gender. You probably know how you feel about all these issues already. You've probably had arguments about them. Arguments that have left you shaking your head in wonder at how anyone could disagree with you. It's simple: we disagree on these things because we have different ideologies. We disagree and it's OK.

So let's take these arguments at face value. Let's not just dismiss those who hold opposing views, claiming they're racist or naïve or elitist, or whatever. Even if it's just for now, I invite you to put your cynical scepticism behind and let's get into the arguments.

Privatisation

Whoop! Privatisation vs nationalisation! Yeah! Sorry, what? That's just me? You think privatisation chat is incredibly dull? Oh. Well, it's not. This is one of the biggest arguments in modern politics. Who runs our services? Our water, our trains, our hospitals? Stick with me here, because this stuff matters.

When musicians release an album that doesn't get much critical acclaim, that the voices in the know say is utterly terrible, they often say the same thing: this album isn't for the critics. If you like what we do, you're going to love this. Well, for many people privatisation is one for the fans. People who like the use of free markets, capitalism, competition . . . those people love privatisation.

But for anyone who doesn't like privatisation, they *really* don't like privatisation. The word itself is tantamount to swearing. They don't like the theory or the practice or the consequences. For them, the argument is lost before it even starts.

And that's the truth of it. There is very little middle ground with privatisation. Most people either love it or hate it.

So let's see if we can understand where each side is coming from and take a look at the basic arguments for and against this most divisive of issues.

The argument for

The arguments that are most used for privatisation are best summed up in a single word: competition. Not the kind you enter in the hope of winning VIP tickets to go and see Ed Sheeran at Wembley Stadium. No, those competitions are all about one person winning and everyone else being faintly disappointed. Admittedly, that's quite close to what people who don't like privatisation say about the process, but we'll come to that later.

Free marketeers say that competition is what makes everyone better. Imagine a football team that only played friendlies. Everyone wants the best results, but if they don't come off, it's not the end of the world. The players would get paid no matter how they played. Nobody would be fired. The media would shrug and say they did their best and that football is just a very hard game to win. There would be no real motivation to improve.

It's only competition that makes football great. All the managers for all the different teams working out how to do things better to get ahead: shifting formations, creating new set pieces, coaching players. With each match it plays, the team gets better and better (in theory anyway). The one that is most effective with its resources, tactics and execution – that's the team that wins.

And so it is with industry. The free market has created a huge range of supermarkets, for example. You might pick one because it sells the best quality food, because it has the best shopping environment, with free coffee and plenty of helpful staff kicking around, or because its products are the absolute cheapest they can possibly be.

Each type of supermarket knows exactly what it wants to be and works hard to be that thing. In recent years we've seen a huge expansion of budget supermarkets. The financial crisis of 2008 really drove this trend. At a time when most people were strapped for cash, certain shops tried to become as efficient as possible to cut their costs and hence their prices. They asked the questions that the major stores hadn't really looked at. Do people actually need the brands they pay more for? It turns out they don't. They're more than happy to spend their money on lookalike products. Do they need lots of staff on hand to point things out? Nope. They can, generally, find what they want. If they're buying good quality food for less money, might they be prepared to queue for a little longer at checkout? Absolutely they are.

Taking all this on board, along with a whole raft of measures the more luxury end of the market would never dream of, the budget supermarkets managed to massively improve their efficiency and steal a sizeable market share from the traditional players.

The argument goes that it's the free market – and competition – that drives this efficiency. People have a choice where to spend their hard-earned cash, so companies have to work out how to attract people to spend it in their stores. The consumer ends up with a wide range of choice – and each choice is better because it has to survive the competition with the others.

At the same time, people in private business are motivated by the profit motive. Every time you make a saving anywhere in your business, you can either pass that on to your customer (which makes them more likely to spend more money with you), or you can keep the money (which makes you and/or your shareholders richer). Both are the aim in this thing we call capitalism. Attracting customers. Making money. Working out how you can change your goods or service so that you can do more of both.

These economic arguments also go hand in hand with the political argument. Imagine you were eating dinner with a big privatisation fan. You've had some soup. Maybe a few croutons for extra crunch. Through carrot-and-orange mouthfuls, your fellow diner has taken the time to explain all these economic arguments. At this point, though, they put down their spoon, take a swig of Riesling, and say, 'But while that's all true, of course – the free market is wonderful and all that – it's the freedom from political interference that makes privatisation really beautiful.'

The trouble with government-run things is that they are run by the government. And there is lots of chat to be had about why time-limited, vote-seeking governments shouldn't be taking the long-term, or even medium-term, decisions for these companies. If you allow them to be autonomous they can do all the things that make them so great. But the main political argument for privatisation is that the people who like the free market the most – we're talking liberals here – want the state to be as small as possible. The state just shouldn't be spending its time doing things that are better carried out by private industry.

The argument against

Those who argue against privatisation take a very different stance. Our national industries, the ones that we all need to get by – power, post, health, transport, water, that kind of thing – aren't the same as football teams. They shouldn't be judged as if they were football teams. Or supermarkets, for that matter. And they simply shouldn't be run by people looking for a profit.

We should be running the water works of the country so that everyone can get water. If we run that well and make a profit? That money should go back into making water even better. Or be siphoned off by the government to pay for other stuff. Better play equipment in schools or something. People simply shouldn't be making money off the fact that we all need to drink, wash and go to the loo. That's not right.

People who don't like privatisation point out that competition is neither possible nor desirable in these industries. We have only one network of pipes to our houses, so we can't use competition and the free market to dictate who supplies the water that comes out of the tap – or who takes it away when it's dirty. The government can run it properly, for the people, but if a private company runs it, without competition they've got a monopoly. They're controlling the game. Sure, some social democrats might talk about legislating to ensure the costs are kept reasonable – but then it's hardly free of government interference, is it?

The critics also point out that the argument that countries can't run things efficiently has been proved wrong time and again – our electricity is partly provided by a government. Not our government, obviously, we privatised it. But 10 per cent of our electricity comes from EDF – Électricité de France. Yes, that's the French government. Running an efficient and competitive energy company. Sorry, what were you saying about needing the free market for dynamic improvement?

You'll remember the socialist theory, too, that people feel better and more satisfied when the fruits of their labour benefit their community. So, why do we need the profit motive to help engineers or managers or whoever work out ways to make things better? We want a more efficient service *for the country*, not to make The Man richer. It's ludicrous, it would be argued, to suggest that making money for the shareholders is more motivating than making something more efficient or being part of a world-class nationalised industry.

And then it comes to money. With the free market, everything is about money. It is prioritised over people. Companies have one job: to make money for their shareholders. They don't care about running gas into your home. They don't care about employing you. Again, the government can legislate here, passing laws that mean workers have to get breaks and the ability to have a wee in an actual toilet, rather than in a bottle so they can get back to work quicker. But a) companies might find a way round them and b) why should we bother? It's like trying to tame a tiger because you'd like to have a cat in your house. It's possible and it might not kill you and eat you, but you're introducing a massive stripey risk into your house. Why not just get a regular cat? Why not keep things nationalised?

When governments employ people, they can do so on reasonable terms, with a living wage and breaks and coffee. Maybe even biscuits. Happy workers work better! Treating people well is good for the people and it's good for the indus-try, which in turn is good for the country. Happy, efficient, hardworking, satisfied people delivering letters or banking or making steel or whatever.

And ultimately some of the industries we're talking about here are pretty darn important in our daily lives. Gas to heat your home. Trains to get to work or visit friends. The internet for getting distracted from what you're supposed to be doing and reading long articles about hyperinflation in Venezuela instead.

These things aren't luxuries. Of course, if we have the money, we should pay for them. But some people don't have the money, perhaps because they're elderly, disabled, unemployed or for whatever reason. If these things were run by the government, they could easily be distributed to those in need.

Finding a compromise

Those are your basic arguments for and against. They are fairly well entrenched and it's hard to see how there can be much middle ground. Sure, some companies are bailed out when things get rocky and are partly nationalised to see them through, like Royal Bank of Scotland, but these are then patched up and sold back off ASAP. We're not talking about brief small-scale nationalisation here. People who support nationalisation want it all the way. Those who love their services with a strong dose of the free market want everything to be privatised. There is no compromise between those two standpoints. You can't be a little bit pregnant.

There are, though, a few compromise measures. You won't be surprised to hear that the social democrats are quite keen on privatisation with regulation. Blair didn't renationalise anything that Thatcher had privatised, despite general Labour outrage at each and every privatisation in the 1980s.

Ed Miliband continued this approach when he was the leader of the Labour Party. In September 2013 he suggested a freeze on energy prices. That's not nationalisation – it's quite some way from nationalisation – but it *is* regulating the market so that you can exploit it while protecting people from the worst ravages of the capitalist system. That's literally the whole game for social democrats.

Of course, he never got the opportunity to make that change. Labour lost the 2015 general election and he was replaced by Jeremy Corbyn soon after. Corbyn is all in on renationalisation. He laughs in the face of regulating markets.

That doesn't mean, though, that the policy was 100 per cent dead. Theresa May came up with a very similar policy to the price freeze. Of course, she called it a price cap and was very keen to point out the differences, but when you get down to it, it's quite similar. The free market, on its own, misbehaves sometimes so the government has to intervene and impose new laws.

In reality, that's not much of a compromise between nationalisation and privatisation. It's just privatisation with a nice frilly bow and strict instructions to behave. Or else.

But there are ways nationalised industries can compete a bit like private companies. Let's look at electricity. Say the government comes up with a new – state-owned – company. It might be called Keep Calm and Power On or something. It starts off providing all staff with fair pay and conditions. Perhaps it tries to reflect the values of the people and make sure the company only uses renewable energy. It could make a point that it never makes a profit – charging people only what they need to pay for the energy created.

Keep Calm and Power On offers itself to everyone in the country as an alternative, nationalised energy company. It would be on all the comparison sites and all that jazz.

Anyone is free to sign up with it if they would like to and there are lots of reasons to do so. It is reasonably priced, it reflects the values of the country, it looks after its workers. We've got something that's simultaneously alluring to conservatives (with all the tradition and support of The County), liberals (people are free to join up or choose a different company) and socialists (who just love the nationalised thing and the workers stuff). Yep. Everyone across the political spectrum is all on board with one plan. What could possibly go wrong?

There may, however, be some issues. All those UK workers cost money – it's much cheaper to set up your call centres overseas. So even though KCPO isn't making a profit, it could be more expensive. The values of a country can change, too. It's very easy for the public to turn away from or embrace certain technologies, but with planning for power plants taking blooming ages, the turning circle for a company can be very slow. It's possible that this vision will be replaced by an expensive alternative that isn't really in line with the national consensus on how to make energy.

So, nobody signs up, which means it doesn't have the economies of scale (that's when things are cheaper because you're bulk buying), which, in turn, makes it even more pricey. All that money you spent on the launch is now an expensive mistake. The politician who started it, with all that pomp and ceremony, finds their career in pieces. They become the punchline on shows like *Have I Got News for You* and *8 Out of 10 cats*. A national joke.

It doesn't have to take that turn. It could work brilliantly. Maybe, though, that possibility of failure is what stops it from happening. Maybe there are just so many risks, it's easier to regulate the market rather than launch into a whole new nationalised experiment. What's important, though, is that there is a halfway house, some middle ground – a way to nationalise without completely removing the free market and all that comes with it.

That's all the theory, but we can see how some of the arguments have played out in real life by looking at some of the privatisations that have taken place in the past few decades – the actual frontline battles over the future of our country.

British Telecom

BT as we know it was created as part of the Post Office in 1980 at a time when demand for phone lines was really hotting up. Everyone wanted a piece of the action. The ability to speak to someone far away was clearly becoming more and more alluring.

The Thatcher government really liked the idea of competition and the free market. She was a big fan of the whole privatisation thing, with as little government interference as possible.

BT became a separate entity from the Post Office in 1981. On 19 July 1982, Patrick Jenkin, MP, made a statement to the Commons in which he said he wanted to privatise the company so that it could benefit from 'access to financial markets' – which means he wanted BT to be able to borrow to invest, but didn't want it to count as government borrowing.

The Labour Party wasn't a big fan of the plan. Its original arguments illustrate exactly the points we've already looked at: the extent to which workers naturally want to work for the good of the country, not the shareholders; protecting vulnerable people who may miss out on the goods if a private company is just chasing profits; protecting the pay and conditions of the workers.

As we know, the privatisation went ahead. And, years later, many people say that it has been a success. Why? Because the company has been a success. It's innovative and has nearly a third of the broadband market. It makes a profit. Most of the country has high-speed broadband access – and it's working on the areas that don't. The combination of the free market, the profit motive, competition and regulation has built a company that does relatively well.

The truth is that it's simply not possible to say more than that. So much has changed since the days when it was first privatised. And we don't have a control experiment. No keyhole into an alternative universe where Thatcher kept it under public ownership. The problem, as is so often the case in debates like this, is that nobody's interested in the middle ground. Fans of privatisation want to paint as rosy a picture as possible. Those against it are only going to highlight the things that aren't going so well. So we're stuck saying, 'Yeah, it looks alright'.

British Rail

In the 1990s, British Rail was deeply unpopular. Passenger numbers had fallen from over 1,000 million a year to under 750 million. Strikes were common place. Things weren't going brilliantly.

When John Major and his Conservative Party won the 1992 election, they had the privatisation of the railways in their manifesto. And so it was they set about introducing competition and the free market into the train system.

The first major change was to create a company, Railtrack, that would run the infrastructure. It owned the track and the stations. They then created twenty-five different slots (which would get reorganised down to seventeen over time) for which private companies had to compete to run the trains.

This is because at any one time, most train lines are monopolies. There is only one train line that visits my home town of Whitstable, for example. It would be hard to have competing trains trying to use the same stretch of track to take me up to London to marvel at the sights and sounds of the West End. Instead, each company would apply for the right to run the line and the one that promised the best service and the most money to the treasury would be selected.

The theory was clear. Get companies competing with each other to deliver the fastest, cheapest (for travellers), most profitable (for the government), most invested-in train service imaginable. These are all the arguments that are always made for privatisation. Allow the free market to work its magic on the trains. Companies like Virgin, Stagecoach, Arriva and others came along to take the government up on these opportunities.

It's interesting to note that Labour fought this while it was going through Parliament, but when Tony Blair became prime minister with a huge victory a few years later, he did very little, at first, to undo any of the changes. Don't forget that Blair was a social democrat – he believed in using the free market to deliver things he wanted. He would have his hand forced, however, a few years into his time as prime minister, by a number of fatal accidents that raised questions about Railtrack. First there was one at Southall in 1997, then another at Ladbroke Grove in 1999. But it wasn't until the Hatfield crash in 2000 that things really started to change. The 12.10 train had left King's Cross for Leeds and was travelling at well over 100 miles per hour when one of the tracks fractured and the train derailed. Four people died.

There were many reports of incompetence at Railtrack. The share price hit rock bottom and the company went into receivership. Many people suggested that the privatisation of the track was directly to blame for the accident. The government then took back Railtrack and rebranded it as Network Rail, which still runs the tracks today – under public ownership.

There are few people today who suggest that the privatisation of Railtrack was a success. As I say, people literally died. Clearly something went wrong along the way. The passenger franchises, though, have been much more of a mixed bag. Again, whether you believe in privatisation really shapes whether you think this one has been a success. In case you're wondering, the Labour Party thinks it's been terrible and we need to take the trains back into public ownership. The Conservative Party disagrees. No surprises there. While Labour points to overcrowding, huge fare increases and profits being paid out instead of going back into the system, the Conservatives counter with the increasing numbers of people who want to use the trains, the range of cheap off-peak fares available and record investment in the network.

The truth, as ever, is almost certainly somewhere in the middle. Some of the train franchises have been successful and made lots of money (to the fury of those who don't like the idea of privatisation, of course). Some have been a disaster. The East Coast Mainline is currently under public ownership after nobody could make a profit on it, highlighting another criticism – that private companies have the opportunity to make lots of money, but there is no risk for them. If things go south, they simply hand it back to the government to soak up any losses.

The final thing it's worth looking at before we move on is the type of nationalisation the Labour Party supports. Labour spokesperson Andy McDonald described it as an 'arm's length' organisation. That's the kind of privatisation where it's effectively a government-run, publicly owned kind of company. The idea is that they are still trying to be efficient, still looking to invest, still driving down costs, but those lovely big profits? They go to the government. There seems to be very little appetite for the return of British Rail.

The National Health Service

If you thought privatisation of the trains was a little, let's say, punchy, you wait till we get into the NHS. The idea of privatising the NHS is just about the most frontline political battle there is.

The front page of a Google search of 'privatise the NHS' comes up with headlines like this: 'NHS privatisation would be "political suicide", says thinktank' (*Guardian*), 'NHS privatisation exposed: Scale of treatment for paying patients at NHS hospitals revealed' (*Independent*) and 'Government is deliberately creating a health crisis to privatise the NHS, doctors claim' (*Telegraph*).

Just the mention of privatisation of the NHS is enough to get people very, very hot under the collar.

The first thing you need to know is what this actually means. It's not like the phone lines or the trains. It's not about a sudden sell-off of the whole organisation. For some of the services that the NHS provides, there is a tender process and private firms can bid to be the providers. So the state decides what needs doing and then finds the private company who can do it the best. Private companies have a look at what's required, work out how much it would cost them and put their bid in. NHS bosses then look at the bids and decide which is the best and who will, therefore, run the services.

People who believe in the privatisation of the NHS think that's great for all the reasons we know they love. The private companies are all about efficiency, cost-cutting and the sweet taste of competition. Those on the other side of the argument object to people making money out of the sick and the vulnerable. They see government money lining the pockets of fat cats. They utterly refute the idea that the public NHS can't do things efficiently.

Just to be clear, then, the privatisation of the NHS is not about ending the NHS core ideal of being free at the point of delivery. 'At the point of delivery' is an important point because in some countries you are charged and then reimbursed, possibly by an insurance firm. That's not what's happening when we talk about privatisation of the NHS. It would still be a system where you pitch up at A&E or go for an appointment or whatever, and will never be charged.

Of course, there are people who want to charge for some NHS services. The NHS is in a bit of trouble, to be honest. The way the whole thing functions is through the working population paying enough taxes to cover healthcare for everyone. But our population is getting older. The number of retired people is getting higher and higher, leaving a smaller ratio of taxpayers covering the bill. The NHS is almost a victim of its own success, too. People are treated more successfully, so they stay alive for longer. The longer they stay alive, the more likely they are to require more NHS treatment.

So, yes, some people look at the financial struggles of our NHS and say that we need to find another way to fund our hospitals, our social care and our GPs, possibly through some sort of insurance scheme, but that is not the argument we're looking at here. We are just looking at private firms taking on certain services within the NHS, without – in theory – having any effect on the people who use it.

How much does it happen? According to the King's Fund (who are experts on this kind of thing), in 2017/18 around 7.7 per cent of NHS spending went to non-NHS organisations (including voluntary sector and local author-ities). That's £13.1 billion.

Let's have a look at one example of a private company, Virgin Care. Richard Branson's healthcare company has bid for lots of contracts. In the period from 2013–18, they received just under £2 billion in NHS contracts. That includes £700 million to provide contracts in Bath and £36 million to provide sexual health services in Teesside. According to their website, since Virgin Care was set up in 2006, it has 'treated more than 6 million people'. That's an awful lot of people. They are a little defensive about taking money out of the NHS, too. Branson has pledged to 'invest 100 per cent of that money into helping NHS patients'.

There are critics of Virgin Care, of course. Many critics. There have been some issues about the company not paying tax in the UK. There was also the time when an NHS Trust in Surrey took back the management of a service, and Virgin Care sued them and settled for hundreds of thousands of pounds out of court. Even the health secretary at the time,

Jeremy Hunt, told the Commons, 'I, too, am very disappointed about the action taken by Virgin Care'.

Jeremy Corbyn is *really* not a fan. In January 2018, at Prime Minister's Questions, he got right into the debate: 'Under this government, Virgin Care got £200 million worth of contracts in the past year alone – 50 per cent up on the year before. The Prime Minister needs to understand that it is her policies that are pushing our NHS into crisis. Tax cuts for the super-rich and big business are paid for by longer waiting lists, ambulance delays, staff shortages and cuts to social care. Creeping privatisation is dragging our NHS down. [Jeremy Hunt] said that he would not abandon the ship. Is that not an admission that, under his captaincy, the ship is indeed sinking?'

Really it comes down to this. Are you, in general, against privatisation? If so, you're gonna really hate privatisation of the NHS. It's the coalface of all the things you hate about privatisation. If you quite like a bit of free-market action, well, you'll probably be in favour of all of this.

And that, ladies and gentlemen, is the truth of all these privatisation examples. The extent to which you think it's going well is largely based on the extent to which you see your life as improved by the presence of the free market. 'Twas ever thus. If you are a fan of McDonald's, you're probably pleased if an extra branch opens up even nearer your house. If you don't like the fast-food chain, you'll probably see its presence as a nuisance. No amount of happy customers will convince you that the opening is a good idea. Our final judgement is based very heavily on our preconceived ideas. That's OK. You don't have to love privatisation or McDonald's or whatever. This book isn't here to persuade you to join the other side. It's just important to understand that the other side also want the best for the country. Whatever your standpoint, you don't have the monopoly on caring about the future of our nation.

Tax and spend

Governments spend money. It's what they do, from schools to hospitals to armed forces. It's something we've all come to expect. If the government declared that it was no longer going to spend money on the police or social care or pensions, there would be uproar. People would take to the streets. Once there, presumably they could do as they pleased, with nobody being paid to keep order. It's a silly idea. Of course, the government need to flash the cash.

The trouble is, they have to get the money from somewhere. And this is problematic. Nobody likes tax. You work hard all month and then The Man takes a percentage of your wage. You earnt it. You got out of bed. You worked hard. Perhaps Adele summed it up best when speaking to *Q* magazine in 2011: '[While] I use the NHS, I can't use the public transport any more. Trains are always late, most state schools are shit and I've gotta give you, like, four million quid – are you having a laugh?'

There are, of course, people who are more than happy about paying tax. People who see it as their duty to not just earn for themselves, but also to work and contribute to the country as a whole. People who look at the things made possible through tax – the NHS, public transport and state schools – with a sense of national pride.

Which means that we've hit another political and ideological battleground. People disagree on a fundamental level and think that those on the other side of the argument are determined to ruin the country.

Those on the left think those on the right are heartless and cruel because they generally want lower government spending and lower taxes. Take this tweet from Jack Monroe in response to claims that the Conservative government was ending its austerity period: 'Give us back our bobbies, our firefighters, our teachers, our rights, our freedoms, our school dinners, our security, our mental health services, our social workers, and fuck off with your budget and your subsidised lives and your stupid soundbite and your wanker briefcase.'

Those on the right think the left are naïve and economically illiterate in their desire for more spending. As Conservative Prime Minister Margaret Thatcher said, speaking on Thames TV before the 1979 election as leader of the opposition: 'Socialist governments traditionally do make a financial mess. They always run out of other people's money.'

Like I say, the left thinks the right are horrid. The right thinks the left are stupid. Sigh.

We're going to have a proper look at these arguments. Of course we are. We're all about mutual understanding and all that. That's how we roll in this book. So let's have a quick recap of the various sides who are all so convinced they are the only ones who are right.

Libertarians

You may remember that this lot are quite big on freedom, and part of that is freedom from taxation. Taxation takes your money away and other people then decide how to spend it. There is no choice here. There is no mutual discussion about what a fair amount to pay might be. There is no consent given. And if you refuse to pay, your liberty can be taken away and you're thrown in gaol. How is this fair?

In the UK there are very few who believe in a zero-taxation system. But UK libertarians are very aware that every penny the government spends must come from taxation, so are adamant that the minimum spend possible should be the aim. Why should someone who has chosen not to go to university pay tax and subsidise someone else's degree? Why should minimum-wage workers pay for a millionaire's healthcare?

The biggest single spend from the government is on welfare. In 2017 that was £252 billion, roughly a third of all spending. For your libertarian, that's a disgraceful figure. People are free – but that means they are free to fail. Sure, you can make bad decisions if you like. Drink. Drugs. That kind of thing. But you shouldn't expect the government to come running to help you sort yourself out.

This extreme conclusion comes from early-twentieth-century liberal William Graham Sumner, who said that 'a drunkard in the gutter is just where he ought to be'. He suggested that the taxpayer shouldn't be burdened with picking him up and sorting him out, because the 'drunkard' has used his freedom to position himself exactly there.

Sumner's position is clearly out of date. These days, very few libertarians would deny the 'drunkard' some help. But many are still in favour of cutting the welfare budget to prevent subsidising 'lifestyle choices'.

(One-nation) conservatives

The Conservative Party has, for a long time, positioned itself as the party of low tax rates. It won the 1992 election partly because of a very successful poster campaign, featuring a bomb with the words 'Labour's Tax Bombshell' above it and 'You'd pay £1,250 more tax a year under Labour'. 'Vote for us and we'll charge you less tax' is a message the party likes.

This falls in line with the conservative ideology and the belief that there is a natural hierarchy. People get paid according to their role and skills, and people who work hard shouldn't have to pay lots of tax to subsidise those who don't work so hard.

Theresa May, as prime minister, has emphasised that the best route out of poverty is work, not just to get paid but to give your life direction and purpose, too. For conservatives, this 'work pays' idea is a the only logical one. Not only does it push people into work, meaning they will pay taxes and contribute to the budget that the government has to spend, but they are also not taking money from the government. Double win. More tax receipts, fewer burdens on the taxpayer. And over time, that allows tax to come down further.

Conservative thinkers also believe in incentivising companies to come to this country through tax cuts. The theory is that the money will then be spent on job creation, helping put more people into work, which justifies the corporate tax cuts.

While conservatives are happy to support those who need it – the disabled, for example – they are intent on ensuring that this burden is proportionate. And as every penny of welfare spending comes from the taxpayer, it's only fair to ensure that each recipient is truly in need and worthy of the money. If someone can work, they should do so, and the government should do what they can to nudge them into doing just that.

Social democrats

Social democrats get out of bed in the morning so that they can marry up socialist aims and the free market. We know that. So what does that mean for tax and spend?

They want to spend money, but they don't really want to tax people very much. They're about being business-friendly as well, which means that big tax hikes for companies are out of the question. The last Labour government found ways to raise money without increasing taxes, such as the PFI initiative, financing spending through business and the free market to achieve socialist goals of equality. That was the idea anyway. You won't be surprised to hear that people disagree over the level of success.

Tony Blair also reformed some welfare payments with his New Deal, intended to end unemployment for young people and those who had been out of work for a long time, getting them off benefits, with 'restart' interviews and 'Work Capacity Assessments', which might not sound entirely dissimilar to the conservative aim.

Socialists

Many socialists ultimately desire a community that doesn't use money at all, one that is based entirely on shared ownership, community and compassion. As such, the idea of what socialists would like in terms of tax and spend is fundamentally transitional, in preparation for an economy for when money is no longer needed.

Socialists want everyone to have a basic quality of life. As such they believe in universal benefits. Everyone has the same needs met and the same opportunities available. Instead of just giving children from the poorest families free meals at school, for example, the Labour Party wants all children at primary school to have a free school meal. This is about far more than just stopping poor children from starving.

There is a big conversation on the left about a universal basic income. That means that the government provides every family with enough to live on, above the poverty line. That's for everyone. People who support it argue that, in one swoop, it would eradicate poverty in the country. All children would get to grow up in a house where there is enough food and heating. It would get rid of some of the gender imbalances, too. Research from the Give Directly charity (which gives money to people in poor areas and allows them to spend it as they need) suggests that spending on nutrition goes up, while spending on alcohol or tobacco remains static.

Even without the basic income, socialists want our public services to be comprehensive. That means the NHS, our schools and universities, the police, transport, housing, and all the rest need to be properly funded.

Of course, this costs money, which needs to come from somewhere. In general terms, socialists aren't against raising taxes, especially for the rich – giving the most weight to those with the broadest shoulders.

We looked at the conservative idea of cutting taxes for big companies to encourage them to invest in the UK and create jobs. Socialists would argue that that simply doesn't work. All that happens is countries compete with each other to attract these companies, and get involved in a race to the bottom, with companies paying less and less tax. You end up with companies not paying anything in return for creating jobs that they would have needed in the UK anyway. Socialists say that this kind of tax break is part of the rigged system, where the richest people – and companies – can avoid tax, but the poor can't.

Socialists believe in taxing corporations and legislating to ensure they can't file their profits overseas. At the 2017 general election, Labour pledged to raise income tax only for the top 5 per cent of earners who are on more than £80,000 per year. They also pledged to raise corporation tax.

Austerity

There we are. The armies on the hill. Giving each other the evil eye. You may notice that I haven't described a liberal army. The truth is, liberals are so split and have such a wide variety of perspectives, that they can align themselves with any of the armies above. There will be people sat round the fires in any one of the camps quietly whispering to each other, 'I mean, this is all fine, but I'm a liberal, yeah?', at which their fellow soldiers will clap them on the back and say, 'Yes, of course you are. You're always welcome here, friend.' Then they'll drink and eat and look forward to the morning's action.

At first light, the sun creeps over the horizon and lands on what is the single biggest ideological battleground in UK politics in recent years. No. Not Brexit. Brexit divides, but not like this. No, the blades of grass on which the dew is gently lifting are on the field of austerity.

Here's a bit of background. Some of this is disputed so I'm going to be as general as possible. Labour spent some money, then there was a global financial crash in 2008. Financial crashes are pretty rubbish for governments. You know those people you've managed to get off the tax burden and into work? Well, all those people just lost their jobs and their houses and their livelihoods. They need government spending and they aren't supplying any money to the taxman. It's expensive and it's sad and it happened. Money ran out.

In 2010, George Osborne became chancellor. That's the person who makes the financial rules. So, in his first budget he said he wanted to eliminate the deficit and reduce the public debt. What's that? I've completely lost you with all this financial nonsense? OK, before we get started here are some definitions.

Debt: Hopefully you know what this one is. It's what you owe people. Or what we, as a country, owe other countries.

Deficit: The amount that we go into debt every day, so if we spend £300 a day and get £250 a day, we would have a deficit of £50.

At the start of the coalition government, the debt continued to grow very quickly indeed. That's because the various austerity measures that were put in place took time to come into effect and every day you're not reducing the deficit, the amount that you are in debt increases.

So, the scene is set. Cameron and Osborne need to reduce public spending. They set about cutting the budgets of almost all government departments. Public sector pay was frozen. Education spending was cut. Social security payments grew more slowly. Almost every single penny spent by the government was reduced.

As we've seen, Labour are split into social democrats and socialists. The social-democrat wing is vaguely on board with Harriet Harman (interim leader of the party in 2015), who instructed the party not to vote against the Conservative Welfare Bill, which included measures such as limiting child tax credits. Harman argued that 'We cannot simply say to the public you were wrong at the election . . . We've got to wake up and recognise that this was not a blip;

we've had a serious defeat and we must listen to why.' Not everybody did as they were told. One Jeremy Corbyn (who was at that point a very unlikely leadership candidate) voted against the bill, along with several others who would become Corbyn's front bench.

In 2015, Jeremy Corbyn took over the leadership of the Labour Party. He set about opposing austerity in every form it took. The battle was now on. On one side of the Commons a Conservative Party whose members self-identify as liberals, one-nation conservatives and libertarians and on the other a Labour Party that self-identifies as socialist.

The gap between the ideologically perfect levels of tax and spend is huge. Uncrossable. A deep, deep chasm. When you throw in the austerity programme as well, things get very ugly.

Corbyn and his team had long called foul on the whole concept of austerity. They accused the government of simply using the economy as an excuse to reduce the size of the state. It's a difficult line for Theresa May to deal with, because of course her party do quite like a smaller state. But the Conservatives don't call it a smaller state. They refer to it as Damian Hinds did when he was a junior minister at the Treasury: 'Everyone benefits from the economic security that comes from the country living within its means.'

The opposition don't call it living within means. In May 2018, Corbyn wrote in the *Mirror*: 'Tory austerity has almost certainly increased the death rate. Today, we can strike a blow against these deadly policies. The full consequences of eight years of cruel and counter-productive Tory austerity are devastating.'

Yep, while Conservatives talk about economic management, Labour talks about cruelty, devastation and death. Many left-wing commentators talk about the 'murderous' austerity programme.

After all the fighting, in 2018 May announced that austerity was over. Boris Johnson went further in 2019, telling the *Spectator* that 'austerity was just not the right way forward for the UK'.

So . . . what does that mean? The battle is over? Has somebody won a decisive victory over what the correct level of tax and spend should be? Is one of the parties having an open-top bus parade through the centre of Manchester? Sadly, no. Not by a long shot. In fact, if anything, the battle has become more intense.

Those on the right generally agree that the Conservatives have done a good job of managing the economy and (excluding spending on infrastructure, which is allowed, because infrastructure building is good for the future) have eliminated the daily deficit. In the 2018 Budget, Philip Hammond, the chancellor at the time, announced he was loosening the purse strings, with extra money for the NHS and even money for potholes and the 'little extras' that schools haven't been able to afford. In PMQs in 2018, Theresa May explained their position: 'Yes, we have had to make tough decisions, and yes, councils have been asked to make tough decisions. The reason we had to do that was because of the state of the public finances and the economy we were left by the Labour government. People have made sacrifices and they need to know that their hard work has paid off. And yes, better times are ahead – under a Conservative government.'

Jeremy Corbyn didn't agree. Obviously. Those on the left are outraged by the idea that austerity can simply be over, without reversing the cuts that had been made: getting more police back onto the streets, allocating more money for schools and the NHS, that sort of thing. Corbyn looked at all the departments where Labour would spend considerably more (and did spend considerably more when it was in government). In that same PMQs in October 2018, he accused her of tricking the country. He finished his questions with this attack on the prime minister: 'Eight years of painful austerity. Poverty is up. Homelessness and deaths on our streets are up. Living standards down, public services slashed and a million elderly are not getting the care they need. Wages have been eroded and all the while, billions were found for tax giveaways for big corporations and the super-rich,' he said. 'The prime minister declared she is ending austerity, but unless the budget halts the cuts, increases funding to public services, gives our public servants a decent pay rise, then isn't the claim that austerity is over simply a great big Conservative con?'

So, there we have it. The ideological battle over tax and spend. And it's being played out right now. We've got two ideological big beasts in charge of the Commons. They disagree so fundamentally and we, as the electorate, as citizens, as people who care about our country, are invited to pick a side. Just don't forget that the other side care too. Please. Never forget that.

Education

So far we've looked at areas where nobody can agree on anything. Deep divisions. Polarised opinion. Accusations of idiocy, cruelty and cack-handedness. And that's just in the Simple Politics office.

It's wonderful to have got to a battlefield where finally we can all agree on something. Are you ready for this? A statement that everyone in the country can get behind? Here we go.

Schools should provide an excellent education for our children.

Et voila! Ça, c'est tout. I'm not going to bore you with the follow-up paragraph in which children are referred to as 'the future'. Because of course they're the blooming future. They're children. That's how time works.

If we all want schools to be kind of ace, what are they doing here in the 'Battlefields' section of the book? Why aren't they in the 'fields of love' section or the 'big, happy, friendly political cuddles' section? I'll tell you why. People mean different things when they talk about excellent schools and an excellent education. Very different.

It's pretty much the same as saying we all want to have yummy food for our tea. Yeah, of course we do. But beauty is in the eye of the beholder and all that.

You probably think you're up to speed on this too. Perhaps you know a teacher. You may even be one. Our nation has around half a million teachers. I used to be a teacher. But even teachers disagree on education policy. We're not a homogenous blob. I've known teachers who are as conservative as they come, as well as all the lefty ones you've probably heard about. I only make this point because you're probably envisaging the teachers you associate your-self with and who you mostly agree with on stuff. That's how friendship works. It's the echo-chamber effect. So, when we're looking at education, please keep that mind of yours open to alternative ways of thinking – don't just shake your head thinking, 'Well, that's not what Jan says, is it?'.

The first thing we need to sort out is the point of edu-cation. We're all well aware of the fact that we should go to school. You now have to be in education or training from five to eighteen. That's thirteen years of our lives at school. If we get our three score years and ten on this planet that's around 20 per cent of our total time. But why do we do it?

According to a speech from Nick Gibb (the schools min-ister at the time and, no, he was never in the Bee Gees) in 2015, the point of school comes down to three objectives: 'Education is the engine of our economy, it is the foundation of our culture, and it's an essential preparation for adult life.' In other words, he wants us to learn how to be workers, how to be adults and how to be, er . . . cultural.

He emphasised the importance of literacy and STEM (Science, Technology, Engineering and Maths) subjects in contributing to the economy. The focus on culture was mostly about reading (with English skills highlighted throughout), with a final paragraph about how schools are also asked to teach music, art, design, drama and dance. The final section on adult life was about 'finding opportunities to instil key character traits, including persistence, grit, optimism and curiosity'.

If this is a Conservative vision for schools, it is clear what they want. Schools are there to give us the skills to be engaged in the economy, as workers and consumers, and teach us how to cope and struggle through when times are tough.

It's noticeable what this vision doesn't include. There is no mention of sex or relationship education when discussing adult life. The word 'physical' pops up just the once – in an anecdote about rugby and the Rugby World Cup delivering programmes for a small number of young people. It's certainly not included as a core part of education. 'Imagination' crops up twice. 'Creativity' not once. 'Skills' is in there nine times.

We should remember that the conservative ideology promotes ideas of tradition and hierarchy as well as modern-day free-market economics. These are good and useful things to help us feel content in our surroundings. Education is there to prepare us for our roles in society. We need to acquire the skills to be the cog in the machine.

If the Conservative vision is about skills for work, the Labour Party talks more about society than the economy. Its policies include things like a free school meal for all primary school students; subsidising nursery places to give children as equal a start as possible; and actively encouraging children to engage in a wide range of activities, such as learning a musical instrument.

While we're here, let's get off the bus for a minute and think about free school meals for all primary school children. It's a beautiful piece of ideological purity. Currently, only children in families on benefits receive a free school meal. Most of us would agree that children who don't have enough to eat at home should be given a free hot and nutritious meal at lunch. Really, that's something almost everyone in society can get behind. Children shouldn't be hungry.

But Labour want everyone to have a free school meal, partly because they think that if some children are on free meals and some aren't, some kind of stigma could develop. One school I've worked in had two lunch queues, one for the free meals and the other for those who were paying. Now, that school had a very high percentage of students on free school meals, so there was no visible stigma in being in the queue for 'tickets'. However, it's not too hard to see that were the ratios a little different, it could be deeply damaging.

It's also about community. It's the act of sitting down and breaking bread together. Physically it ensures everyone has a decent meal, but spiritually it means we come together and are bonded by our shared experience. This is socialist gold. They love it.

What about those of a more conservative persuasion? On the one hand, they are big fans of encouraging community, building those bonds together in a way that gets you to buy into society. A free school lunch for everyone, though? That's going too far. The state – the taxpayer – would be paying for a free lunch for someone who can easily afford it. At PMQs Theresa May has often remarked that every penny of government spending is taken from the taxpayer. Those struggling to make ends meet should never have to pay for something for the child of a millionaire. Incidentally, this is the same argument that is used for subsidising people to go to university.

Back to the socialist vision for schools, then. The concept of universality also percolates through the Labour ideals in other ways. They aren't keen on private schools. That's a level of segregation and separation that they just can't really get behind. They want to make private schools pay full VAT – adding 20 per cent to their costs and, presumably, forcing many children back into the comprehensive education they value so much. The same is true of academies and free schools. In short, they want everyone to go to local schools together, sharing the same experiences and forming the kinds of bonds that create a cooperative and communal society.

These things shouldn't be surprising. Conservatives follow conservative ideals. Labour follow socialist ones. But what about social democrats? If this were a clickbait article, I'm sure I would start with: 'You'll never guess what Tony Blair and David Blunkett did to education!' But I'm sure, by this stage, you can guess. They attempted to introduce free-market choices in schools.

The Labour government of 1997 to 2010 allowed schools to specialise in different things and parents got to choose which school to send their offspring. They had helpful things like league tables and school inspection reports to help them decide. Schools that were struggling would have useful and timely interventions to help them improve.

And there were brand-new types of school that could enter the market too. City Academies (later, just academies) were like regular schools, but with no local-authority connection. They could buy services from anywhere they wanted. They had a bit more freedom around the curriculum and over whom they chose to hire as teachers, so they could hire experts in history, rather than necessarily someone with a teaching qualification. In short, the heads had more flexibility to do the things they saw as essential to improve the school – and had fewer bits of red tape and hoops to jump through to do so.

Oh, yeah, that's competition making everything great. Again. The sounds of those high fives can still be heard echoing around the Department for Education.

Grammar schools

Perhaps it's because I live in Kent, which is one of the areas of the country that still has multiple grammar schools, but it always feels to me that the most ideological of education battles is over grammar schools.

Here's the basic argument for grammar schools: young people take a test at the age of eleven to see what flavour of school suits them best. We're all different, so trying to lump everyone together in a single school is probably a terrible idea.

The test is all about basic aptitude. Schools (well, state schools) aren't allowed to teach students how to do the test. The idea is that everyone who takes it is coming in blind. They have to do some maths, some English and some reasoning. If you get a high enough score in all three (individually as well as a total score) you're clearly one of the most intelligent children. No regular school for you. Nope, you're off to grammar school. It's not quite the kind of place you can only access through a special platform at King's Cross, but it's pretty darn special. There you will receive the kind of education that was completely out of your reach at a comprehensive, surrounded by all those thickos. You'll receive more of a classical education, too. Latin is on the cards. Strings of GCSEs and A-levels await. Entry to some of the UK's (or the world's!) top universities is in sight.

That last one – about universities – is really important for fans of grammar schools. You see, it's all about social mobility. Working-class children who are a bit special can be saved from the drudgery of comprehensive education and sent off to a place where many more doors are open. It's been described as talent spotting.

At the party conference in 2019, Boris Johnson spoke about increasing social mobility through education: 'The best way to level up and to expand opportunity is to give every kid in the country a superb education, so that is why we are levelling up education funding across the country.'

That's the point. In the Conservative ideal, where we live in a meritocracy, social constraints won't stop you from achieving your goal. Nope. We've got this system that can lift you out of the role that your parents may have filled. It doesn't matter if nobody in your family has ever gone to university. We'll take you in, we'll support you, and you can go all the way to Oxbridge and the world.

Those who didn't make the cut will go to secondary moderns. These schools will offer skills-based training to match the abilities and aspirations of people who probably aren't going to go to Cambridge. They focus more on vocational courses, apprenticeships and supporting students when it comes to the core subjects of English, maths and science. These schools are in no way less good than their grammar equivalents. They are just different.

There we go. That's the argument for grammar schools, backed by parties on the right. The Conservative Party backed expansion of grammar schools in 2015 and in 2017. UKIP went further. It wanted a grammar school in every town, saying that when the system was in full swing 'grammar schools improved social mobility by giving children from poorer backgrounds access to career paths they might have previously thought out of their reach'.

But, of course, those on the left don't agree. Their dislike of grammar schools is so strong that leftie journalist Stephen Bush described them as 'the horror-movie monsters of public policy – they have been shot to pieces by almost every serious policy thinker from across the political spectrum, and yet they stagger on regardless'. Labour has been talking about getting rid of grammar schools since the 1960s.

Here's why. According to Full Fact, a fact-checking organisation, poorer children are less likely to go to grammar schools. That whole thing about social mobility? It doesn't happen. In 2016, 17 per cent of children living in areas with grammar schools were eligible for free school meals. But just 3 per cent of the children attending the grammar schools were eligible. Grammar schools simply weren't taking their fair share of children from poor families. And in any case, socialists don't want to encourage any sort of separation within the education system at all – they want all children to have access to a comprehensive education, but everyone should be part of the same system.

It's not just that poorer students weren't getting in. The Institute for Fiscal Studies says that 12 per cent of those at grammar schools in Year 7 (the first year of secondary school) hadn't attended a state school in Year 6 (the last year of primary school). That compares to 2 per cent of all Year 7 students in all state schools in England. In short: a lot of school places in the selective school are going to young people who have been privately educated at Primary level.

Which means that the young people who are hoping to be talent spotted may be passed over, with their places going to students from private schools. That's not encouraging social mobility. That confirms and perpetuates class divides. Which, let's remember, isn't something that socialists are particularly keen on.

Life isn't black and white, though. Let's not forget here that some students *are* plucked from families living in poverty and get to go to grammar schools. And those children do seem to perform better than they might have done in a comprehensive. Going back to the IFS, 'There is robust evidence that attending a grammar school is good for the attainment and later earnings of those who get in'.

Yes, they do go on to say that 'there is equally good evidence that those in selective areas who don't pass the eleven plus do worse than they would have done in a comprehensive system'. There is that opportunity, though, for the brightest and the best to get into grammar school.

Is it worth it? You know what I'm going to say here. It's entirely up to you to decide which side you agree with!

Immigration

So far, these battlegrounds have been all about the ideologies. Different ways of thinking that affect the way we see solutions to the country's problems. Immigration is a special case, though. Immigration is so often about things that aren't really to do with immigration at all.

We need to get something out of the way first. Racism and xenophobia. These things exist. Some people don't like other people because of the colour of their skin, or because they are different in some other way – a different language or life experience, perhaps. It's irrational and negative and prejudiced and utterly awful.

One of the points of this book is that it's OK to have alternative opinions to other people. Not just OK. Marvellous. It's one of the things that makes this human experience quite so exhilarating and interesting. The rich tapestry of political opinion. But as soon as your ideology is about proclaiming the inferiority of other people, mindless hatred and instinctive prejudice, it's no longer just about different opinions. You have lost the right to be taken seriously and should be challenged.

There is a lot of discussion at the moment about giving people with these views a platform. Indeed, later in this book we'll discuss freedom of speech. There are some people who go out of their way to shut down any debate or talk given by people whose message lies in hatred of others. That's not what I believe in. I believe in debate and winning the argument. Exposing people as negative, irrational and just wrong.

Anyway. I'm not going to discuss racism again in this section. I believe that the vast majority of people aren't racist. As a country we're better than that and far too many accusations of racism are thrown about. But there are certainly a lot of people not keen on immigration, so if it's not down to racism, what's going on?

According to three polls by the company YouGov, taken in 2016, 2017 and 2018, we think we have too much immigration in this country – 63 per cent of people thought that in April 2018.

One stark difference is in class. In this immigration poll, middle-class people were 32 per cent less likely to say that immigration is 'much too high'. In short, working-class people are more likely to dislike immigration than middle class people. That attitude was also reflected in the 2016 Brexit vote. According to another polling company, Ipsos

MORI, more than 60 per cent of the working class voted to leave the EU. It's generally accepted that one of the driving forces of voting to leave was the issue of freedom of movement – people were uncomfortable with the levels of immigration into the UK.

Age also plays a significant part in the way people feel about immigration. Back in that YouGov poll, 80 per cent of those aged 65+ thought that immigration is too high. That's almost double the 41 per cent of 18–24-year-olds. The people who were most likely to vote to leave the EU were 65–74-year-olds, 66 per cent of whom ticked the 'Leave' box.

In short, it looks like older working-class people are most likely to have an issue with immigration. To understand why, we need to look at what people are talking about when they talk about immigration. Don't forget that in this I am making the assumption that almost everyone isn't racist and it's therefore nothing to do with them not liking the people who have moved to our country.

Before we look at that in detail, I just want to clarify some distinctions between different types of immigrant for anyone not up to speed on these things. Immigrants are people who have moved to the country to live. The term includes everyone, from the French family who moved to Putney to work in financial services to the Syrian family fleeing from a warzone.

Refugees (sometimes called asylum seekers) are immigrants, but they are a specific kind of immigrant who are literally seeking refuge in our country. They have fled their home because they could no longer live there, perhaps because of a war or a natural disaster, or because they are personally facing some kind of life-threatening discrimination, maybe because they are part of the LGBTQ+ community, for example. According to the UK-based Refugee Council, there are over 68.5 million people around the globe that have had to flee their homes. In 2017, according to the United Nations High Commissioner for Refugees, the UK was home to 121,837 refugees.

The term economic migrant is often used to describe people who have come to the UK in order to make more money and have higher living standards than they could in their home country. This is often because the pound is so strong. Many people can earn more in the UK working in the fields, picking fruit or harvesting broccoli or whatever, or cleaning offices and people's homes, than they can working in their area of expertise back home. A lawyer, for example, might be able to earn more picking gooseberries in Ashford, Kent, than they could working in their profession in their home town of, say, Riga, Latvia. Professionals moving to the UK to further their careers are also included in the term economic migrant. The governor of the Bank of England, Mark Carney, is a Canadian living and working in London. He's an economic migrant too. As members of the European Union, anyone from another country in the EU could come to our country to live and work.

So, why are so many people, especially older working-class people, anti-immigration?

First off, many immigrants arrive in the country with very little. They therefore settle in areas that have high levels of poverty. And that's where we start to see why some older working-class people are uncomfortable with high levels of immigration. They've seen their home towns turn from a community they understood into an area with many more residents than the area was planned for. When there is a sudden influx of people, facilities and services become overstretched. That means the schools are full. The hospital is full. Simple things like getting an NHS dentist appointment become tricky. That's nobody's fault. It just takes time for an area to adjust and open new schools, expand the hospitals. But the money to expand all the services is often hard to come by. Poorer immigrants are unlikely to pay much in tax.

Where there are high levels of immigration from a certain area, they may well bring aspects of their culture with them. In many places now, for example, there might be more than one 'Polski sklep' – a Polish shop selling delicacies from back home, with bold, bright colours and slogans in Polish advertising their wares. Again, for the people who have lived their entire lives in the area, this can feel like a big change. Suddenly there are shops that are explicitly not for them.

The high street that once felt so familiar has become slightly alien. This is also, it should be noted, taking place against a background of shops struggling on the high street. The combination of out-of-town complexes, the 2008 financial crash and online shopping means that many shops lie empty, making the unfamiliar shops more noticeable.

Then there are the immigrants themselves. Now, there is no suggestion that they aren't nice people. They're people. Some will be lovely, some may be a bit irritating. That's life. But the demographics of these migrants aren't typical. A lot of the work that is abundant is manual labour, on construction sites or in fields. That means that lots of the people who have moved are young(ish) men, who are sending money back to their families, and the population of these areas has become asymmetrically male. Again, there is nothing inherently wrong with men. It's just a change in the demographics of the area that, again, can leave some people feeling a little adrift.

When people from areas like this talk about being anti-immigration, that's what they are talking about. They're talking about lack of resources, oversubscribed local facilities and a rate of change that is unfamiliar and alienating. Which is why it's about older working-class men.

Young people have been brought up in this environment. I taught in inner-London schools where in the average tutor group of thirty or so young people, the majority would speak a different language. Many of today's twenty-somethings have grown up in much more diverse communities – particularly in large urban areas – with a higher level of immigration and a faster rate of change than the older generations experienced. This is the country they know. Sure, some are still saying migration is too high. There are many reasons for that. The resources thing is one. No matter how used you are to living with people from all over the world, nobody wants to wait six weeks for a dentist appointment. There is also an issue for school leavers facing increased competition for jobs. Again, it's not really about the people. It's about jobs and funding for services.

One way to show that this is not necessarily about where people come from or the colour of their skin is that almost everyone wants workers for our NHS. The YouGov poll showed that 86 per cent of those aged 65+ were happy with current levels of immigration or wanted more immigration of people to work in the NHS, and 72 per cent of working-class people wanted the same. As a nation we love our health service and are happy for anyone to come here and help sustain it. By way of comparison, just 23 per cent of those aged 65+ were happy with current levels or wanted more immigration of people looking for low paid work. That's a pretty big gap.

The middle-class experience of immigration is also entirely different. For them, the software designer from France who has moved into number 23 down the road is most welcome. He brings with him a comfortable level of exoticism, the opportunity to dig out what you remember from O-level French. Meanwhile, the working-class migrants supply labour. They clean homes, fix your plumbing and sell you flowers. Middle-class areas aren't struggling with services in the same way. No wonder middle-class people are so much less likely to say immigration is 'much too high'.

These tensions over immigration are hugely problematic, partly because many people complain they can't talk about levels of immigration without coming across as racist. They feel like they are walking on egg shells. People who are terrified of describing someone as 'black' in case it's somehow misunderstood may find it very hard to articulate that the lack of GP appointments in their area is something to do with immigration. That leaves people in a difficult situation. How do they express their discontent? There is a fear of 'the elites' looking down at them. Sneering. Accusing them of prejudice and bigotry.

It's one potential reason for the Brexit vote, as people felt they were able to have a say on immigration for the first time. There is a narrative among 'Remain' supporters that many (working-class) people voted for Brexit because they wanted to get rid of people from Pakistan. This is a Remain joke, because obviously immigration from Pakistan has absolutely nothing to do with the European Union. The truth is that many people did vote for Brexit because they are uncomfortable with levels of immigration. And, yes, it's possible that some of those immigrants are from Asia, and their immigration status has nothing to do with the EU. This was an opportunity to vote about immigration, though, and some people took it.

Immigration is also an ideological battleground. The Ipsos MORI survey found that Conservative voters were 40 per cent more likely to say they think immigration is too high. Does that fit with conservative ideological thinking? Absolutely. They want to protect British traditions, values and culture. Again, it's possible that immigration is getting the blame for things that aren't its fault. The rate of change and the erosion of that sense of Britishness can be attributed to globalisation and the Americanisation of our culture as much as immigration, but the newcomers to our country seem like an obvious place to start apportioning blame.

Likewise, there are ideological reasons for the Labour Party to be more likely to support current levels of immigration. Socialism can be very internationalist. It promotes the idea that workers are equal regardless of nationality. During the Scottish Independence Referendum of 2014, the socialist politician George Galloway toured Scotland with a message that Scottish workers have more in common with the workers from the North of England than they do with the ruling class in Scotland. A pamphlet created for the tour said: 'Two and a half thousand years ago Socrates declared that he was not an Athenian or a Greek but a simple citizen of the world. Albert Einstein described nationalism as an illness, the measles of mankind . . . It sickens me that the country of my birth is threatened by such obsolescent dogma. Flags and borders do not matter a jot.'

In short, those coming to our country, whether to flee persecution or to make a better life, are coming to us as workers. The Labour Party is, in theory, the party of the worker. The issue it has had is that the country has been more anti-immigration than the party, so there was a time, before Jeremy Corbyn was the leader, when it tried to show how tough on immigration a Labour government would be. In the 2015 election, the party released a lot of mugs on which was printed: 'Controls on immigration. I'm voting Labour'.

Even now, there is still tension in the party as to how pro-immigration they should be. While they are staunchly pro-worker, there is also a sense that they are pro-British worker first. In March 2018, Corbyn told the Scottish Labour Conference that he wanted to be able to take steps 'preventing employers being able to import cheap agency labour to undercut existing pay and conditions'.

Possibly the biggest ideological gap around immigration is about people's behaviour when they reach our island. Should they be assimilating into our British way of life, or should they be free to continue with their own customs? There is a particular ideology that is relevant here called multiculturalism and it's all about plurality. People coming together from across the world and living cheek to cheek. Different languages are spoken, different religions are practiced, different food is prepared, different traditions are honoured.

In a liberal world, this allows everyone to carry on as they would like. In the UK, we have churches following a variety of flavours of Christianity, from the Church of England to Russian Orthodox. We've got synagogues, temples, mosques. We've got restaurants and cafes serving food from across the world. On our buses and our high streets, we hear people speaking every language under the sun.

This is a system where everyone's culture is equal. There are no prizes awarded for following the traditions of the host country. People are free to come and stay within their own communities, not learn English and rarely leave a fixed geographical area that is likely to feature a high number of people from a similar background. Alternatively, they can assimilate if they would like, taking parts of their own culture and blending them with Britishness.

In the 1960s, 70s and 80s, many people warned about the impact of immigration and multiculturalism. In 1968, the MP Enoch Powell made a famous speech, known as the 'Rivers of Blood' speech, in which he spoke of people who 'found themselves made strangers in their own country'.

In 1990, Norman Tebbit spoke of a loyalty test for migrants, telling the *Los Angeles Times*: 'A large proportion of Britain's Asian population fail to pass the cricket test. Which side do they cheer for? It's an interesting test. Are you still harking back to where you came from or where you are?' He picked up the same theme in 1991, saying that some immigrants don't integrate 'because some of them insist on sticking to their own culture, like the Muslims in Bradford and so forth, and they are extremely dangerous'. This ideological standpoint is the opposite of multiculturalism, concerned instead with preserving the idea of Britishness. When you think about the one-nation conservative ideology, which is all about keeping the best of our past to build the future, it's clear that multiculturalism is a challenge.

Things changed, however as the years went on. The 1997 Labour manifesto (which would see the party win with a landslide public vote) included the line: 'Britain is a multi-racial and multicultural society. All its members must have the protection of the law.' Despite many of the core Labour supporters being wary of immigration (for the reasons we've just looked at), Blair introduced several pieces of legislation that were, either wholly or in part, about protecting the rights of migrants and migrant culture. These included the Human Rights Act in 1998 and the Race Relations (Amendment) Act of 2000.

We have remained a liberal country, with no restrictions on worship or language or anything like that, but in 2011 Prime Minister David Cameron spoke out against multiculturalism: 'Under the doctrine of state multiculturalism, we have encouraged different cultures to live separate lives, apart from each other and the mainstream. We have failed to provide a vision of society to which they feel they want to belong. We have even tolerated these segregated communities behaving in ways that run counter to our values.' He went on to blame multiculturalism for the radicalisation of young Muslims and extremism on all sides.

Cameron wanted people to sign up to ideals that he believed a 'genuinely liberal country' would 'actively promote'. These were 'Freedom of speech. Freedom of worship. Democracy. The rule of law. Equal rights regardless of race, sex or sexuality.' Theresa May made comments along the same lines in 2015 when she was home secretary: 'When immigration is too high, when the pace of change is too fast, it's impossible to build a cohesive society.'

The issue of immigration raises a lot of ideological questions. What should our country look like? How many people should we be taking in? When they come here, how would we like them to behave? What do we offer them? What is more important, personal liberty or 'a cohesive society'? At what point do you suspend people's freedom to act how they want? Everyone is in favour of civil liberties and all of that, until, well, until they aren't. Until something happens that they don't want to happen. I've always quite liked AFC Wimbledon, they are a reflection of how great football fans can be, they've started from scratch and they're generally pretty great. But. If my team were playing them in the Cup? If their direct aim was equal and opposite to my direct aim? I'd want them to lose. And many people find this with the idea of immigration and British culture. They're happy to support the former until they think it threatens the latter. And where people draw the line depends on their ideology.

Ultimately, it's possible that multiculturalism comes up against the same issues we're going to look at in the next section of this book: freedom of speech. So it's time to leave the subject of immigration, but, to get you thinking about freedom of speech, have a go at these questions: what should we do as a society if one particular culture wants to, say, subordinate women? Is it liberal to allow them to do so, or is it liberal to try to, in some way, liberate women in that culture? What would you do? Where is your line?

Free speech

When we talk about other countries, we're always very much in favour of free speech. It's an absolute no-brainer. We rush to condemn attempts to suppress it, particularly in those countries we believe we are better than, as is clear from a couple of recent-ish headlines: 'China must abandon censorship' (*Guardian*), 'China congress: How authorities censor your thoughts' (BBC), and, in the USA, 'Beijing hinders free speech in America' (*New York Times*). The outrage and moral superiority are everywhere.

It's not just in the media. When Google tried to amend its search platform, so it would be allowed to operate in China, its own workers were up in arms. Distraught. This was not what they had signed up for when joining Google. I mean, sure, the gyms and volleyball courts and gourmet food and massages and all of that – they're the main reason to work for Google – but apparently there is also some kind of belief in spreading information and promoting freedom of expression.

In 2010, the Nobel Peace Prize went to someone called Liu Xiaobo, for exercising his right to free speech as a poet and literary critic of China. Except that, as we've seen, freedom of speech doesn't really exist in China, so Mr Liu received the prize while in prison.

In the West we've been fans of freedom of speech for a long time. This used to be about protection from the monarchy and/or government. Way back in history, James II wasn't a big fan of people saying not very nice things about him and rather took it out on Parliament. So, in 1689, after he had been deposed, the Bill of Rights was introduced to protect those in Parliament and enable them to speak out against monarchs in future. Exactly a hundred years later, the French Revolution handbook *The Declaration of the Rights of Man* referred to the importance of freedom of speech in allowing people to criticise the state and not be prosecuted for so doing.

In 1941 – a rather important time for American politics, with the Second World War well underway, but Pearl Harbor still eleven months off – Franklin Roosevelt gave a speech to congress saying: 'to a world based on four essential freedoms . . . freedom of speech and expression . . . of every person to worship God in his own way . . . freedom from want . . . freedom from fear . . .' Sorry, Mr President, what was the first freedom you spoke of? Ah, yes. Freedom of speech.

Today, in the West, freedom of speech isn't so much about criticising the state. We pretty much take that for granted. It's about social freedom to express your views, however salty they might seem to the people around you.

So. Section over, right? We all think freedom of speech and the freedom of expression is important and we're all proud that it's a pillar of British values. It's important to us and the only question is over these dastardly foreign countries. Why can't they be more like us? Why can't they be more liberal, with people free to say what they want, when they want?

Except, of course, that this just isn't true. While almost everyone will say that we should have freedom of speech, what that actually means varies wildly.

Ideologically speaking, the group most in favour on this topic is the libertarians, of course. Don't forget that if you're a libertarian you are all about freedom. When you hear the first strains of George Michael, you're running towards that karaoke booth, screaming 'Freedom!' Maybe you change the words a little to reflect the role of civil liberties. Why? Because you can. Not for you the tyranny of those lyrics scrolling at the bottom of the screen. You do what you want when you want. Stick it to the karaoke man.

Then you've got your conservatives. While they may not be quite as forthright in this game as their libertarian compatriots, they see freedom of speech as a British value. And what do conservatives like more than anything? A British value.

Talking in the Commons in December 2016, Sajid Javid (secretary of state for housing, communities and local government at the time) said 'My hon. Friend highlights the importance of promoting British values and making sure that they are accepted by all communities in Britain. That includes tolerance, freedom of speech, freedom of religion, respect for democracy and so many other things. The more we can do to make sure that every community embraces those, the better off we will all be.' Safe to say, he's a fan.

So far, so un-battlefield-like. Libertarians and conservatives agree. It's time to introduce a dissenting voice. Because love of freedom of speech is all very well until you begin stress-testing it. Until people start to say things you really don't like.

And this is where we are with those on the left. They're behind the idea of freedom of speech all the way – until they're not. Nobody is trying to censor us every day, not in the way that China is accused of doing. But socialism isn't a liberal ideology. It doesn't say do what you want. It says you have a duty to do what is best for your community. So sometimes socialists say no, it's not OK to say that.

This viewpoint has led to initiatives like creating safe spaces at universities. These are particularly common in America but have increasingly been adopted in the UK. The Edinburgh University Students' Association, for example, say they operate under a 'Safe Space Policy which covers all Students' Association spaces and events'. The policy goes on to state that the aim is 'to create an environment in which all students, staff and visitors feel welcome, respected, and able to fully participate in our events and activities. It sets out our collective commitment to the principles of liberation, equality, diversity, and inclusion which we place at the heart of everything we do.'

How is this safe space created? It's through a zero-tolerance policy on certain behaviours. If these behaviours aren't stuck to, you could be given a verbal warning, asked 'for an Acknowledgement of Wrong-doing and Apology', or you could be kicked out of the venue. The policy is very clear, and it encourages people to report violations.

Here's a list of some of the behaviours banned from the safe space:

Harassment – which is here defined as 'any behaviour which is directed at an individual or group which is non-consensual.'

Abuse – 'covering both verbal and physical abuse, including sexual assault, which results in an individual or group feeling intimidated or unsafe.'

Discrimination – including verbal and physical expressions of discrimination based on a long list of attributes, including class, gender, religion, trans status and political affiliation.

Violence – 'any act of physical intimidation or aggression, including threats of violence.'

There then follows a vaguer set of bullet points, asking people, among other things, to 'be aware of the connotations of their language', 'avoid making assumptions about another person' (again followed by a long list of specifics), and be prepared to be challenged and 'to learn from the experience'.

The Students' Association of Edinburgh University has specific, written policy that impacts on the freedom of speech. You are not, in one of their spaces, free to use language that might make other people feel intimidated. Note the emphasis here: it's not about what the speaker means, but how the receiver interprets the words.

The idea here isn't to repress people's speech. Not at all. It's to provide a level playing field so everyone can get involved and feel positive about themselves and their surroundings. It's about making us equal and making sure everyone has a say.

Within the Safe Space movement, people sometimes demand that entire events be cancelled. Many Safe Spaces don't want people to enter the university who might contravene their safe space rules. Germaine Greer is a feminist who has some forthcoming views on trans women. She believes that even if someone has an operation to remove their male genitals, they still 'can't be a woman'. She made comments along those lines in the autumn of 2015. She was then the subject of much protest and a petition calling for her not to attend a lecture she was going to give at Cardiff University.

So, this is the stress testing of the freedom of speech vibe. Germaine Greer has spent decades writing about gender roles. She has some opinions about trans women that some could find offensive, in some way denying them the right to define their own gender. To be fair, she's got some views on quite a few things that people might not like, but it was this one in particular that people objected to. In the end she did give the lecture, but people still protest at her public appearances.

This is the heart of the argument – people might feel discriminated against, or even verbally abused by, the proponents of certain views. It's better, therefore, that they stay away and don't upset people who are trying to manoeuvre their own way through this human experience. The right to not be upset, in some specific settings, is now deemed more important to some people than the right to freedom of speech.

It's not just Germaine Greer, either. Various others have fallen foul of the no-platforming in recent years, including

George Galloway for expressing controversial views on what constitutes sexual assault, human rights campaigner Maryam Namazie for her stance against religious laws, and gay rights campaigner Peter Tatchell – for supporting freedom of speech in the face of the no-platforming trend.

It's not actually a new idea, although its aim seems to have changed. The more extreme left elements have been trying to shut down those on the extreme right for quite some time. A group called Antifaschistische Aktion were active in 1932 in Germany. Initially they were mainly a communist group, although some social democrats would later join to try to combat the rise of fascism. They weren't altogether successful.

In 1972 the National Union of Students tried to stop any National Front members talking at their universities, but that was about combatting what the union saw as racism or fascism, rather than protecting individuals from what they might feel is abuse. Incidentally, the 'no-platforming' of people considered racist or fascist is still the policy of some groups. Anti-fascist, or Antifa, activists regularly attend speeches in the hope of shutting them down. Anne Marie Waters, who left UKIP to create her own political party 'For Britain', and Tommy Robinson (or Stephen Yaxley-Lennon) are two regular targets.

Back to safe spaces. This is where the battle really is. Because on the left you've got a faction calling for a space where we are listened to, acknowledged and protected, while those on the other side, the libertarians and the conservatives, think all this is nonsense. They think the presence of these safe spaces risks destroying the concept of universities. They call the students who are protected by these safe spaces 'snowflakes', a reference to their fragility (melting easily). They believe that this drive to protect everyone from being offended in any way shuts down debate, stops people from being exposed to, and engaging with, alternative points of view. That people take offense far too easily, and, really, it's just a way of preventing others from voicing opinions that don't chime with their own. As Theresa May said during PMQs in 2016: 'I think everybody is finding this concept of safe spaces quite extraordinary. We want to see that innovation of thought taking place in our universities; that is how we develop as a country, as a society and as an economy.'

This is a topic that MPs have become increasingly worked up about. Between 1986 and 2017, freedom of speech wasn't discussed once by MPs. Since March 2017, it has happened three times, including a full debate in Westminster Hall (the second debating chamber, like Court Number One at Wimbledon). Very few MPs attended in support of safe spaces.

But while most people might not want to shut down debate, the issue does raise another question about where exactly we draw the line between spirited debate and hate speech. What is acceptable to say, and to what extent should we allow people to spread hate about others?

The truth is that in the UK there are limits to freedom of speech – and these are generally supported by mainstream politicians of all flavours. Theresa May, again at PMQs, told the Chamber: 'There is a balance that we need to find. We value freedom of expression and freedom of speech in this country – that is absolutely essential in underpinning our democracy – but we also value tolerance of others and tolerance in relation to religions. This is one of the issues we have looked at in the counter-extremism strategy that the government has produced. Yes, it is right that people can have that freedom of expression, but that right has a responsibility too, which is the responsibility to recognise the importance of tolerance of others.'

Yes, she wants a balance. And what do we definitely know about finding a balance in political battlegrounds? It's very, very hard to do.

What frequently comes up here is the idea of political correctness. There are many people who believe that they can't discuss certain things – race, ethnicity, sexuality – at all. They're terrified that they will be labelled racist or bigoted or whatever else. As we saw with immigration, these are often older people who may not have grown up in such multicultural surroundings. At some point, many people got the message that to refer to someone's ethnicity is a Bad Thing. People feel that they always have to watch their language and what they say. And they hate it.

The impact of this is almost entirely negative as people take advantage of this sense of political correctness gone mad. In 2001, for example, after being criticised for his comments on immigration and multiculturalism, BNP leader Nick

Griffin wore a gag over his mouth and a T-shirt that said 'Gagged for telling the truth' at the general election results in Oldham West. His policies explicitly talked about protecting our culture and were widely regarded as racist. And yet he had just received thousands of votes. His colleague was wearing a T-shirt that said 'The voice for Oldham'.

The narrative that the establishment doesn't want you to hear something is always compelling. The defence here is always freedom of speech too. Nick Griffin is no longer a figure on the British political landscape – in fact, the BNP itself has almost disappeared. In the 2017 general election, they fielded just ten candidates, down from 338 in 2010. But there are still people who hold these sorts of views, and a great many of them support a man who calls himself Tommy Robinson.

Tommy Robinson uses the 'freedom of speech' line again and again. It's his go-to argument. He too believes that there are issues with multiculturalism in the country, but it's his particular focus on Muslims that really sets him apart from mainstream UK politics. He regularly wants to discuss what he calls 'radical Islam'. In 2017, he broke the law in the way he reported on a court case. For many cases, details can't be published in case the jury is influenced by how a story is presented. If you break these rules, it's called contempt of court. Robinson saw that as an offence to his freedom of speech. He went into a court at Canterbury, recorded the proceedings on his phone (which is also illegal) and described the defendants – who had not been found guilty of a crime at the time – as 'Muslim child rapists'. In 2018, while under suspended sentence for the offence, he did a similar thing again in Leeds and this time was sent to prison. There were various 'Free Tommy' campaigns started by people who support his version of uncovering the truth – in effect the same message that Nick Griffin was trying to send in 2001. Gagged for telling the truth.

Here in The Breakdown, the issue of free speech – who is 'allowed' to speak and when – is increasingly becoming a part of our lives. That's partly because, as we know, we're all happily bumbling along in our echo chambers, oblivious to the arguments of others. Champions of our own perspectives. These little corners of the world that we build for ourselves make the idea of shutting down others very simple. 'Hey! That's not what I think! Stop!' Those trying to express their dissatisfaction with the state of affairs feel ignored and become ever more dissatisfied, only willing to listen to people who agree with them.

And that can lead to more extreme views. Ideas don't sound so radical when they are drip-fed to you on a daily basis and your friends online all agree with you. Way back when it was Nick Griffin on the front line, you needed to turn up at rallies to meet people happy to discuss these things. Now? You're only a click away from finding all sorts of people on the internet, active on social media, ready to agree with you, to join you in your echo chamber. There are fewer dissenting voices present to challenge the more extreme views being exchanged. And so people on both sides become more and more distant from those they disagree with.

In short, then, freedom of speech is a thing everyone likes. In theory at least. What limits you might like to put on it, where you choose to draw the line between freedom of expression and inciting hatred of others, depends, largely, on your starting point.

Brexit

One of the things about a book is that, once it is published, it's done. The wonderful Persian poet Omar Khayyám wrote about events and time passing: 'The Moving Finger writes; and, having writ, Moves on: nor all thy Piety nor Wit Shall lure it back to cancel half a Line, Nor all thy Tears wash out a Word of it.' You can't go back and change things now.

And so it is that, by time you have this book in your hands and are reading these words, Brexit may no longer be an issue. It may be a battleground of the past. A relic of history. You may have a half-baked memory about a time when parties and Parliament and the public were tearing themselves apart over the UK leaving the EU. 'I'm so glad we're out of those dark and troubled times', you might think to yourself as you shake your head and reminisce.

Or maybe not. You might be reading this to try to make sense of a world where Brexit is still dominating politics, the news and everything else. You may be hoping that this section can in some way help you through this whole debacle.

Either way, what I can't do is explain today's particular squabble. I can't come and hold your hand and tell you that everything will be OK, that somehow we'll come together as a country behind *something*. That's because this is a monu-mental battleground. Many people have many different perspectives on what we should do as a country. And these visions are so diverse that trying to find a compromise can feel utterly impossible.

Some commentators say that Brexit has permanently destroyed our political system. The two biggest parties are irreconcilably torn in two (or four or eight or sixteen . . . thirty-two . . . etc). The public is simultaneously outraged, confused and, well, bored. It's an impressive combination.

You want evidence for that? In 2018, one of the most cel-ebrated voices of the Brexit debate came not from a politician or a journalist, or even from a distinguished politics simplifi-cation organisation. No. The most lauded contribution came from documentary and soap star Danny Dyer. On Thursday 28 June, ITV's *Good Evening Britain* had a surprisingly mixed panel. Jeremy Corbyn, Pamela Anderson and Danny Dyer were all present and correct. You may have been forgiven for assuming that Corbyn would do the politics. And maybe he did. Nobody remembers. Because it was all about Mr Dyer.

Danny Dyer launched into a rant about Brexit that col-ourfully captured that potent mixture of confusion, boredom and frustration that so many people feel (you'll have to excuse the language here, he's got a potty mouth that man): 'Who knows about Brexit? No one has got a fucking clue what Brexit is. You watch *Question Time*, it's comedy. No one knows what it is – it's like this mad riddle that no one knows what it is, right? So what's happened to that twat David Cameron who called it on? Let's be fair . . . How come he can scuttle off? He called all this on. Yeah? Called it on. Where is he? He's in Europe, in Nice, with his trotters up, yeah? Where is the geezer? I think he should be held to account for it. He should be held to account for it.' Then, just as it felt like he had finished and the conversation would move on, he spat out the final insult: 'Twat.'

The acclaim with which this rant was greeted speaks volumes about the way the country felt in mid 2018. Not just from Remainers (although there is a clear Remain leaning here), but generally by people from all sides who had had enough. People were sick of hearing about it. The troops had all been engaged in hand-to-hand combat for so long, it wasn't even clear who they were fighting, who their particular enemy might be, or even how they got into the fight. So how did we get there? How had this issue so spectacularly split the whole of British politics and society? To understand this convoluted battlefield, we have to go back to the start.

In 1952, six countries (Belgium, France, Holland, Italy, Luxembourg and West Germany) formed the European Coal and Steel Community. It wasn't sexy. It allowed those countries to trade freely in the coal and steel that they all needed in order to rebuild after the war. They soon realised they'd quite like to trade other things, too. I mean, how much fun can you really have with coal and steel? So they changed the name to the European Economic Community (EEC).

Initially, in 1957, it was still just those six countries, but the idea of all that free trade soon attracted other countries, like bees to a particularly nectar-y flower. On 1 January 1973, along with Denmark and Ireland, the UK joined the fun. Jimmy Osmond was at number one in the charts with a song called 'Long Haired Lover from Liverpool'. *Last of the Summer Wine* was just about to air on TV for the first time. What a time it must have been to be alive.

The first European referendum, however, didn't take place until two years later on 5 June 1975. The Labour government, under Harold Wilson, said that it would recommend voting in favour of continued membership. That didn't mean that Labour's official policy was to stay in; in fact, it had no official position on the matter. This allowed the party to survive the disagreements on the left over EEC membership. The Conservative Party was also very flexible with its MPs, but Margaret Thatcher, leader of the Opposition at the time, was firmly in the 'Yes' camp, along with the majority of Conservative MPs.

It's amazing to look back at the divisions of the time. Those arguments about the EU that we're having today? Well, a whole lot of them were out in force through the spring of 1975. The quotes and campaigns will feel very familiar to anyone who has even vaguely followed politics since 2016. The chair of the 1922 Committee (a group of all the backbench Conservative MPs, which has a certain level of power to shape the leader's position) at the time was a man called Edward du Cann. He spoke out against the Labour Party, saying it was 'hopelessly and irrevocably split and muddled over this issue'. Yes. 'Irrevocably split'. Remind you of anyone today? It's interesting to reflect, though, that du Cann himself ended up supporting the 'No' camp, announcing his decision in the week before the poll.

The 'Yes' team campaigned on security – one of the areas that Remain focused on as well, forty years later. Sure, it was with more of a post-war vibe, but the similarities are still there, with poster slogans such as 'Nationalism Kills' and 'No more civil wars'. Trade was the other focus, pointing out how well stocked the shelves would be and the array of choice that would become available. These were arguments that united the majority of the 'Yes' camp. And they were largely in agreement. That's because it was supporting the status quo. We knew what being in was like, because we were already in. Much like in 2016.

Unlike the more recent referendum, however, the 'No' camp was also fairly united, with politicians from opposite ends of the political spectrum coming together. It seems amazing now that Enoch Powell (a former Conservative minister, but now with the Ulster Unionists) and social-ist stalwart Tony Benn shared a platform. They argued that the EEC wasn't really about trade at all but about the creation of a 'superstate'. They worried that we would be consumed by an EEC that would take away sovereignty and that the overall benefits would be outweighed by the sacrifices demanded. Tony Benn said, 'Britain will be gov-erned by a European coalition government that we cannot change'. One of their slogans was 'Out, and into the world', promoting the idea of trading more with Commonwealth nations. These arguments really haven't changed much over the years.

Given the whole Brexit thing today, you've probably gathered that in 1975 we voted 'Yes' to staying in. It was a huge victory: 67 per cent to 33 per cent. Over 17 million votes for and around 8.5 million votes against. Looking back with the benefit of hindsight, this may seem surprising. As with the 2016 election, both main parties mostly advocated staying in, as did banks and what we'd now call big business. And yet, the result was very different to 2016. Perhaps people had more faith in the establishment back then. Perhaps Brexit really is down to the Leave campaign's incredibly intelligent use of social media adverts. Or, perhaps, when it was purely an economic area, the EU was more attractive to UK voters.

I'd love to tell you, dear reader, that that's where the story ends. We had a bit of a national conversation. We decided that we'd stay in. Everyone shook hands and got on with their lives. But, of course, we all know that's not what happened. The 'No' camp didn't just disappear.

We did see a lull in the conflict, though. Relatively speaking. The 1980s saw Greece, Portugal and Spain all join, making the average temperature of the EEC considerably warmer. It wasn't until 1992 that the Conservative divide really came to the fore. It all started in a small town in Belgium called Maastricht. The birthplace of the European Union.

The Maastricht Treaty was all about turning the trading block of the EEC into something much more, 'creating an ever-closer union among the peoples of Europe', centralising power and moving some areas of power away from individual countries to Brussels. And this was when many of the more right-wing Eurosceptics really stepped up to the plate. They hated Maastricht. They hated it a lot. They also had quite a bit of power, because the Conservative Party had only narrowly won the 1992 general election. Major had a majority of twenty-one.

Three countries (France, Ireland and Denmark) gave the people a say. Tensions were pretty high in France, for example, where 'Dit non à Maaschricht' became a rallying cry for the anti-establishment movement. France voted to stay in, but only just – the result was 50.8 per cent to 49.2 per cent.

The UK didn't have a referendum, but that didn't mean it had an easy ride, and again some of the similarities to 2016 are uncanny . . .

In 1992, John Major, and many of his Conservative colleagues, thought that it would be beneficial for trade and security, saying: 'I believe that the Maastricht agreement protects and promotes our national interest.' But those that didn't like it argued that it gave away too much power. Have a think about conservative ideology. Two of the things that matter to Conservatives are tradition and a sense of Britishness. There is an inherent mistrust in anything that challenges or might dilute this sense of Britishness, including the way we choose to run the country. Parliament is and should be sovereign, MPs should only be accountable to the electorate. The term 'take back control' wasn't specifically used, but, yeah, it's not too far off. Oh, and one of the big rebels in the

Lords? The man who took John Major to court to stop us from signing up to the treaty? Lord Rees-Mogg, father to current Brexiteer Jacob.

Then there was the more libertarian element in the Conservative Party. The free marketeers. They thought that the EU would undermine free trade, creating taxes, barriers and regulation and all the things they hate.

There were many on the left who believed in the EU machine, citing jobs, human rights and collectivism, but plenty opposed the treaty as well. They saw it as an establishment that sought to allow big business and the bosses to exploit the workers. The EU has very little democratic accountability due to its size. The workers would have no chance against this machine of the establishment. Tony Benn spoke against the bill, questioning the transfer of powers away from Parliament and to the government, meaning the government would be free to sign treaties without the authority of Parliament. Benn said that this would take the power away from the people. At one point in the beginning of the bill's journey through the Commons, Scottish socialists in the Labour Party, John McAllion and George Galloway, tried to stop the whole thing as a point of order that Scotland was being denied its democratic rights.

So, John Major had the job of enshrining the treaty into UK law. In order to do so he had to win a lot of votes. The bill started off in May 1992 and was given a hard run. The result was so close that both parties brought in MPs who were decidedly unwell in order to cast their votes. Official

Labour policy was to abstain in the final vote in 1993, but 66 voted against it, while 5 voted for it. Eventually the bill did make it through Parliament with 292 votes to 112.

But, again, those who opposed the treaty didn't just go away. Some of their names may be familiar to you from our current Brexit fun and games: Iain Duncan Smith, Liam Fox and Alan Duncan were among the rebels.

This was when we really saw that both the Labour Party and the Conservative Party were split on the issue. And they have never quite come back together again.

Anti-European voices from the conservative and libertarian traditions grew louder and louder. UKIP formed in 1991 as the Anti-Federalist League, and by the 1994 EU elections it was ready to stand. The party didn't get all that many votes, but it managed to become the fifth largest party in total. It then had to contend with James Goldsmith's Referendum Party, which was, as you've probably worked out, campaigning for a referendum in the EU. Only one of UKIP's 194 candidates managed to get over 5 per cent of the vote and retain his deposit. That candidate was a man called Nigel Farage.

It's fascinating to note that so many on the Brexiteer side were finding their feet in the 1990s, and over the next few years those figures grew in popularity and status. Jump forward ten years and we have the twin machines of UKIP (now under leadership of that man Farage) and the Eurosceptic arm of the Conservative Party both campaigning hard for another referendum.

The European elections of 2014 saw a victory for UKIP – the first time a party other than the Conservatives or Labour had won an election since 1906. That year also saw Conservative MPs who disliked the EU defect to UKIP, emboldened by its success. There was a feeling of momentum under their wings.

With the rise of both groups, then Prime Minister David Cameron attempted to hold the Conservative Party together by making a manifesto promise in the 2015 general election that, if he won, he would call an In/Out European referendum. He won the election and on 20 February 2016 he announced that there would be a referendum on 23 June 2016.

The rest, as they say, is pretty much history. There were campaigners for Leave from across the spectrum who didn't like the lack of accountability, the centralisation of power, the threat to our pillars of British democracy. Those who wanted to Remain – which, as in 1975, was the official position of the government – wanted to protect the trade and security that we had built up over the past forty years. The arguments were made. The people voted. I'm sure you don't need me to remind you what that result was, but, just in case, 17.4 million people voted to leave, while 16.1 million voted to remain: 52 per cent to 48 per cent. We voted to leave.

There are many people much cleverer than me who talk about that vote and discuss the reasons for it. For me, one thing is clear: those who wanted out had been rehearsing their lines for decades. If not quite since 1975, definitely since 1992. They were passionate and committed to the goal of bringing the UK out of the EU. They could stand on stage and bang that drum about sovereignty, independence and trade with the Commonwealth and other growing nations (remember that 1975 slogan? Out and into the world? Yeah . . . that).

At the same time, those who wanted to remain couldn't be quite so unequivocal. Nobody in the world thinks that the EU is a perfect and flawless organisation. Remainers think that, despite some flaws, the UK is better off being in. Which, well, it's just not such a vote winner. 'On balance, I think this' isn't as persuasive as 'I've been campaigning all my life against this evil thing that we must now leave'. We're also living in a time of anti-establishment feeling. People don't like to do what they are told to. We're all against The Man and in 2016 it was very clear that The Man wanted us to vote to stay in the EU.

The trouble was, all those Leave campaigners didn't actually agree on anything other than leaving. So after the vote, when we tried to work out what leaving would actually look like, the trouble really started. The libertarians want nothing more than free trade with the world. They're, generally, quite happy with the idea of a no-deal Brexit. Out and into the world. Again. The conservatives want to keep our traditions, but also want to maintain some of the existing trade arrangements. Let's not forget how pragmatic conservatism can be as an ideology. A deal is pretty essential for them. Those on the left want to ensure that Brexit doesn't reduce human rights or have a negative impact on jobs – a deal is important to them, but not the same type of deal as the conservative Brexiteers wanted.

Which is why we are where we are. A confused and muddled battlefield. People coming at the debate from all sides of the political spectrum, and everyone wanting something very different, which makes a compromise very hard – perhaps impossible – to find. This may take quite some sorting out.

Gender roles

This battleground is a tricky one to write about. When we talk about gender, absolutely everything means something. The very language we use can be deeply offensive to some people. The whole thing is an absolute minefield. Don't believe me? Just search the word 'gender' on Twitter. Go on. Do it now. I guarantee that you'll find all sorts of people promoting their own vision and concept of gender, and a whole bunch of angry threads disputing every single one. It's the ongoing battle of the ages.

We're going to have a tour around all the things that different people think. You're going to disagree with some of them. I can't promise not to write something you don't like. It's a sign of how hotly contested this issue is that I need to put in my own caveat here. Please forgive me if my own language strays into an area that you feel is in some way wide of the mark. No disrespect or offense is intended, I promise.

We've already had a very brief look at gender roles in this book when Theresa May described 'boy jobs and girl jobs', which might still sound like a pretty remarkable thing for the second female prime minister of the country to say. But some people – largely restricted to the conservative ideology – do still believe in traditional gender roles. It often comes down to some kind of biological determinism – for example, the idea that most men are physically stronger than most women and are therefore naturally more suited to some jobs. They don't see gender as a barrier, exactly, just as a guideline to help you find the roles you can excel at.

But most people don't accept these sorts of definitions of gender roles any more.

The biggest single movement in gender roles over the past however many years has been the advance of feminism. Feminists look around at our society and they see a world that isn't fair. A world that makes life easier for men, in which men are paid more money; are much more likely to run a big company; and tend to make most of the laws.

This is something feminists call the 'patriarchy': a cosy world created by men for men, in which women can only perform certain roles. They can be the carer (supporting people through cooking, cleaning, that kind of thing), the mother (strictly speaking, I guess this is part of the carer role, just a super specific strand) or the mistress (alluring and sexual). When feminists protest against the idea of having 'boy jobs and girl jobs' it's because they see those 'girl jobs' as conforming to the roles that the patriarchy has assigned to women. The work women do is much more likely to be unpaid, and when they do get into the workplace, they are paid, on average, around 10 per cent less than men.

Feminists would say that there are all sorts of subtle ways the patriarchal system is promoted across our society – things that might seem harmless at first but actually play a part in reinforcing traditional roles and stereotypes. The pen company Bic, for example, produced a pink pen under the 'Miss Bic' brand and labelled it 'For her'. It cost more than the regular Bic pen. In the *I* newspaper's Christmas 2018 gift guide for teenagers, there was a girl section and a boy section. The boy section featured a bicycle helmet, a go-pro outdoor camera, sporty trainers and an indoor skydiving adventure. The girl section? Sequin mini-skirt, jewellery, a selfie-taking kit and a hat emblazoned with the slogan 'Hello Gorgeous' on it. The assumption is that boys want to go out and have adventures, while girls only care about their appearance.

These are two fairly trivial examples of the patriarchy at work. But there is a darker side. According to the Office for National Statistics, in the year ending March 2017, 180 women were killed, 90 of them (50 per cent) by a current or former partner, an average of roughly two a week. There were, admittedly, more male homicide deaths, but only thirteen of them (3 per cent) were killed by a current or ex-partner.

One in four women experiences domestic violence. In the year ending March 2018, 1.3 million women in England and Wales reported experiences of domestic abuse. 1.3 million. I'm not saying for a second that men don't suffer from it as well. They do. But they are approximately half as likely to be victims.

Feminists say the patriarchy shapes and prods and manipulates girls from a young age, forcing them to accept the roles they are given, and to see themselves in a certain way. They live in fear of the physical dominance that their male friends, colleagues and neighbours could exploit. Feminists say that the dice are loaded, that the odds are stacked against them. Subtle ways of reinforcing gender roles allow the patriarchy to perpetuate itself. Take, for example, the fact that women MPs are so outnumbered by men. Possibly because the vast majority of MPs are male and have historically been male, the idea of what an MP looks like in our heads is likely to be male (and white, but that's a conversation for another time). With that picture in our head, it is possible that we're less likely to vote for a woman, who doesn't fit that image.

If many feminists agree on what the problems are, the same cannot be said of the solutions. That's a battlefield in itself. Partly because while some problems would seem to have a relatively easy fix, others are not so straightforward. Take the pay gap, for example. It may be possible to draw up legislation that ensures every big organisation pays men and women the same wage. These companies already have to publish their gender gap. To require them to publish it and then adjust wages as necessary isn't beyond the wit of man.

(There I go. 'The wit of man'. It's not a saying I just made up, it's a relatively common phrase, but what it does is use the word 'man' to stand in for 'everyone' or 'people'. It's not 'beyond the wit of people' still works, you'd still get the idea. But that's not what the saying is. The regular and repeated use of phrases like this, feminists say, is another example of how the patriarchy is deeply rooted in our society.)

Anyway. Apologies. We could force companies to pay all genders the same wage. What about the gift ideas, though? Could we force the *I* newspaper to print gift ideas that tell our young women that they can be adventurous and active and all the rest of it? Or boys that they can focus on looking nice and taking selfies – don't forget that it's not just women who are oppressed by the patriarchy. Boys, too, are forced into certain roles, with expectations of resilience and toughness – what is sometimes referred to as toxic masculinity. So, that gift guide traps everyone. But what on earth would the legislation look like to stop gift guides supporting stereotypes? That doesn't sound very plausible to me.

At the same time, there are many schools of thought in feminism, and each strand has different solutions. By and large all feminist groups call for equality with men, but beyond that there are all sorts of ideas flying around. Feminism isn't attached to any one of the ideologies that we've been looking at. A bit like how every MP and every member of the public had their own vision for Brexit, feminists are a wide-ranging bunch of people. They sometimes have different responses to even the most basic of questions. Let's take a quick look at women's bodies. Is it a feminist act to show off your body, maybe even manipulating the male gaze? Kim Kardashian would probably say it is. She uses her body to dominate social networks, to create a brand and ultimately to make a lot of money.

What about people who work as prostitutes or in the pornography industry? Are they exploiting male desires for their own gain, or are they exploited by men in the most visible form of patriarchal dominance?

What about women wearing the hijab? Should we tell them not to, because they're being exploited? Or should it be up to the person wearing it? Can the hijab-wearer make a balanced decision when they've grown up in a patriarchal world that has been all they've known?

Generally, feminists' ideas fit with their regular vision of the world. Liberal feminists are, well, you've probably guessed this, liberals. Marxist feminists are . . . Marxists.

Let's start with libertarians. We know what gets their saliva glands pumping, right? Individual freedom. So what kind of feminism do they advocate? Individual freedom. Women fighting for their own rights, refusing to do what they are told and making their own way in the world. Sod the rules. Powerful, independent and strong women, doing it for themselves.

How about those one-nation conservatives? Surely they don't consider themselves feminists? Actually, that's exactly how they describe themselves. In autumn 2015, Labour MP Rupa Huq asked David Cameron, at PMQs, if he was a feminist and, very kindly for us, Cameron explained exactly what he meant by feminism: 'If feminism means that we should treat people equally, then yes absolutely.' He went on to say how 'proud' he was that women made up a third of his cabinet.

That's a pretty great little speech there for understanding a conservative feminism. He wants people to be treated equally, but note that he makes no mention of introducing legislation or using his office to change the way that women are treated. It's actually quite similar to the libertarian idea of individual feminism. Except it relies on something conservatives are very keen on – the idea of family and community. Cameron wanted something called the Big Society – where individual citizens took it upon themselves to improve their area. So it's up to people in their own communities to treat women equally.

That he said women should be equal and then declared proudly that a third of his cabinet was female perhaps shows the length of the road ahead before equality in representative politics is there.

So, Cameron called himself a feminist. What about Theresa 'boy jobs and girl jobs' May? You bet she does. While she was home secretary she wore a T-shirt that said 'This is what a feminist looks like'. It's the slogan of a feminist pressure group called the Fawcett Society. Speaking in early 2012, years before she became prime minister, the then minister for women and equalities told *Total Politics* magazine (which is, alas, no more): 'It's that age-old question that some people don't like the term "feminist" because they think it portrays a certain type of woman . . . To me, it's about ensuring there's a level playing field and equal opportunity.'

That's actually fairly similar to Cameron's view, although it does suggest that it may take more input from Westminster to help in the battle for equality.

May's feminist credentials came to the fore again during the battle to become the new Conservative Party leader. Conservative MP Ken Clarke referred to her as a 'bloody difficult woman' (he maintains that he didn't know his microphone was on, but he's such an experienced professional, I'm afraid I don't believe him for a second; he knew what he wanted to tell the world about Theresa May). This was a label that she picked up and ran with, and has used it several times since, including warning EU Big Shot Jean-Claude Juncker that he would find her 'a bloody difficult woman'. The Fawcett Society even made a new T-shirt printed with the slogan.

Again, we see the conservative vision for feminism falling not too far from the libertarian tree. Individuals fight for their own particular corner of freedom and equality. Maybe it's a case of libertarian feminism +, with the plus being a desire for all women to be treated equally with men. Which nicely fits the one-nation idea of everyone coming together. One of the current Conservative Party slogans is 'a stronger, fairer country with real opportunity'. It could definitely be argued that there are some feminist ideals in that.

Those on the left, on the other hand, don't trust society. We know they think the goose is already cooked, that left to its own devices, society will always tend towards oppressing vulnerable groups – including women. So, they very much want to take concrete steps to stop this from happening. To borrow from the Labour slogan: to protect the many from the few.

Socialist feminists believe that women are being deliberately exploited for their unpaid work at home. It's just another way in which the bosses and owners of the means of production can squeeze the life out of society and ensure that the workers are too tired and too busy to rise up against their exploiters. The most extreme form of this, often associated with Marxist feminism, is revolution. Rise up against the male oppressors. Create a better world.

That's not, at the moment, a mainstream perspective. Much more popular is ensuring that women are given a chance. Not just hoping that through some kind of osmosis women's rights will naturally sort themselves out. That means making rules to stop companies from paying women less; setting quotas for women on boards; and helping women around the world. In March 2018, Jeremy Corbyn announced a new international aid policy that was 'explicitly feminist', promising to reduce inequality, not just poverty, around the planet.

We could go on here. We could go through radical feminism (which involves completely re-shaping society to be almost entirely led by women), anarcho-feminism (anarchist vibes), postcolonial feminism (moving feminism on from its predominantly white membership – there is a concept called intersectionality that suggests there are a multitude of ways that people can be oppressed – as in class, gender, race, sexuality etc – and they are all happening simultaneously and can't be considered in isolation), and lots and lots of other different flavours of feminism, with lots and lots of ways of combating the patriarchy.

This book isn't about taking sides, though, so it's important to look at the flip side of the feminism coin. We need to talk about 'menism'. People who think men are being left behind, that men are struggling for equality. Menists find the constant promotion of feminism to be oppressive. The great fanfare, for example, of International Women's Day is always anathema to them. Sure, there is an International Men's Day too, but that just doesn't carry the same weight.

Hang on, you might say, what could men possibly say was stacked against them? Let's have a quick look: 76 per cent of suicides are men; 60,000 fewer boys than girls go to university every year; 85 per cent of rough sleepers in the UK are men. It's not just the rough sleeping either. In 2018, of the 597 homeless people who died on the streets or in temporary accommodation, 501 of them (84 per cent) were men. Men are less likely to report their struggles, either mental or physical. Men are more likely to be sent to prison – and for longer. Remember that protest group Fathers 4 Justice? Members used to wear superhero outfits and climb on roofs of famous buildings. Their campaign says that courts don't give fathers enough access to children, that the automatic position is to give custody to the mother.

The obvious comeback to this is that men rule the world and run the businesses, but the argument is that we're talking about a tiny proportion of men. The vast majority are the workers, who have been taught that boys don't cry and that they just have to get on with it. We were talking about domestic abuse earlier in this section and, yes, a third of domestic abuse is against men. But men don't like to report it, because it feels a bit rubbish, possibly a bit weak, to admit that you are being abused by your female partner.

There aren't the kinds of divisions in the menist field that there are in feminism. It's too small for that. The battle that many menist campaigners say they face is for their complaints and problems to be heard and not ridiculed. They feel that, because we're so overrun with feminism, society doesn't recognise them.

It's worth saying that socialists see all of these issues as part of a deeper problem with capitalism. The issues faced by both men and women are all caused by a system that pits them against each other in the fight for profits and status; a system that was never designed to help the poor and the vulnerable.

However, the battlefield of gender and gender roles isn't just about women's rights or even men's rights. The battleground attracting the most attention in the gender sphere at the moment is the issue of trans and non-binary gender. The idea that we can all self-identify as whatever gender we feel we are. This is the fight over trans rights and it's very bitter.

Some people feel that they are a different gender to the one that they were assigned at birth. They don't want to be, say, a man. This isn't about sexuality. It's not about whether they want to have sex with someone of their own gender or not. That's a distraction. It's about how they feel deep down. I'm not going to get into the biology here, I'm not an expert. It's just something that some people feel.

Perhaps the most logical thing to do is to say, 'If that's the way you feel, no worries. You're now a woman'. To let people use whichever pronouns they like, be it she/her, he/him or they/them. Nobody wants to deny anybody their feelings and negate their right to be whoever they want to be. Sure, there are some conservatives who may raise an eyebrow, but even most of them would probably say that if a person feels repressed, or even depressed by their assigned gender, they should feel free to change it. At that level most would say it's nothing to do with them and be more than happy for people to do what they want. Sure, it's not how things were a few decades ago, but we're in a very different world.

Some people may struggle to deal with this level of change, and so this particular battleground may be more generational than ideological. People used to joke that judges and other high-ranking professions would be 'Linda' at the weekend, or would secretly wear ladies' underwear. Such attitudes have ill-prepared that generation to discuss trans issues openly and sensitively.

The issue, for some, is when implications arise of being a trans woman, possibly with no biological treatment or changes. There are people who call themselves trans-sceptic. They say that it's not OK to declare yourself a woman and then have access to the various female-only spaces. You see, over the years we have made many things available to women only. Sports, prisons, toilets, we even have women-only halls of residence at university. These spaces tend to be for women to fight back against the patriarchy or to level the playing field. At the most basic level, they are places of physical safety too.

Some members of the trans-sceptic community criticise the idea that someone could benefit from all the male privileges growing up, but then encroach on female spaces as if they were an equal. They suggest that there is an unfair biological advantage for those who spent most of their lives as a man. Some of this came to a head in October 2018. A transwoman called Rachel McKinnon won a world championship cycling race. She has not had surgery but had been on a testosterone suppression programme to make her eligible. Different sports have different criteria for when you can compete in a women's race. Cycling has a maximum testosterone level. If you're transitioning from a woman to a man, you're good to go immediately.

There it was for some trans-sceptic people and campaigners. A man winning a women's race. The end of women's sport as we know it. Campaigners were putting up posters and stickers declaring that 'women don't have penises'.

While for some, the victory of Dr McKinnon was a step too far, for many others the debate that followed (and, to be fair, the debate that has been raging for a few years now) was deeply offensive. The word 'trans-phobic' is regularly used for people who speak out against the fluidity of gender identity. Those 'women don't have penises' posters? Merseyside Police looked into making them illegal as hate speech. The argument goes that there are people who, biologically speaking, were born male but now identify as women – so these signs are denying them a basic right. Trans people have just as much a right to identify their gender as anybody else.

Let's go back to Rachel McKinnon. Clearly lots of people said she had an unfair advantage over the rest of the field. Self-publicist and attention-seeker Katie Hopkins tweeted about 'a febrile madness' (to be fair, it's an excellent use of the word febrile – the signs of a fever – I do like it when people use excellent words, especially in a controversial moment). The woman who came third replied to Hopkins' tweet saying 'I was the 3rd place rider. It's definitely NOT fair.'

McKinnon herself then took to Twitter to defend herself, saying '3rd place (Jennifer Wagner) claims it's unfair for me to compete. At Masters Worlds, she beat me in the 500m TT. She beat me in 6 of 7 races at the 2017 Intelligentsia Cup. In 2016 she beat me in all 3 Speed Week crits. She's won 11 of our 13 races . . . and it's unfair? Excuse me?' She went on: 'This is what the double-bind for trans women athletes looks like: when we win, it's because we're transgender and it's unfair; when we lose, no one notices (and it's because we're just not that good anyway). Even when it's the SAME racer. That's what transphobia looks like.'

The truth is that this stuff really matters. It really matters to the trans people themselves because they feel the need to express and identify their genders. It matters to people who describe themselves as trans-sceptical (and others may call trans-phobic), because they see it as an erosion of the female spaces that they cherish. It matters to yet more people because they just want a clear and easy solution to this, but there is no middle ground between the first two camps. There can be no compromise. A transwoman is either a woman or she is not. If she is, then surely she must have access to the female spaces. If she's not, then you're denying someone the right to express themselves in a very important way.

The arguments are difficult. In autumn 2017, a transwoman, Karen White, was transferred to a women's prison. She was on remand for rape and sexual offences against women. While in prison, she was accused of four sexual assaults against women, at which point she was transferred to a men's prison. The logical inconsistency here is troubling. If she is a woman she should be in a women's prison. Do other women who assault other prisoners get moved to male prisons? If she isn't a woman, and belongs in a men's prison, what on earth was she doing in a women's prison? This battleground is so intense and so complicated that we can see the authorities making it up as they go along.

That's why it looks like this particular battleground is only just starting. It's not necessarily related to the traditional ideologies we've spent most of this section discussing. In fact, there are many people who don't hold particularly strong opinions on this. For many people it's just about wanting to get it right. What's the correct opinion here? Can women have penises? Is it OK for people to declare themselves a woman? What pronouns should we use for people? If you're not already strongly for either side of these arguments, it can feel very difficult to navigate your way through them.

Sure, there are those who have been making these arguments for years, decades in fact, but the public is slowly waking up to them in a big way. Don't expect this to go away.

PART THREE

Making Change Happen

We've now spent quite a long time together. We've looked at various ways people think, and the things that matter most to different people. You know that some prioritise freedom while others are more into equality vibes. We've been through a few of the key battlegrounds in modern politics. With any luck, you're now feeling more confident about making your way through this messed-up world. And, hopefully, you're just that little bit less likely to shout at someone at a party if they express views with which you disagree.

That's an important step. It's the kind of tolerance that our country is founded upon. A strong British value, if you will. So, well done you.

Even I must accept, though, that you aren't interested necessarily in politics just so that you can have a tolerant and respectful conversation with a stranger at a party. No. You're interested in politics because you want to see change happen. You want to make the world look more like it does in your dreams. You want to take the small steps – or even the big steps – to see a transformation in the way the country works. Or maybe not even the country, perhaps just your town. Your community.

As we've seen, the way most people become engaged in politics is through immediate issues with which they are concerned: the fire at Grenfell; Universal Credit; fear of/ excitement for a Corbyn government. And yes, I can see that if you're fired up about something like that, you're after more than just being able to better understand the arguments for grammar schools that your Auntie Jean keeps going on about.

Right now, then, we're moving on to how people make change happen. We're not going to focus on arguments from either side on this, or whether a particular change has been positive or negative. We're just going to look at how individuals can put their ideas into action.

Individuals can have a big impact. When I was at Parliament's Education Service, I saw a group of A-level students question Labour MP Peter Hain (now Baron Hain in the House of Lords) about which of his achievements he was most proud of. He paused for a second and then asked if it would be OK to reply with three things. The students acquiesced, so he gave the following list: his role in the end of the apartheid in South Africa, his role in the Northern Ireland peace process, and the minimum wage. From anyone's perspective, that's quite the list. He wasn't claiming full responsibility for any of them, but that's not the point. Nobody can make change happen singlehandedly. It's not how the system works. But you can certainly make a difference. There are steps you can take to help turn your vision for the country into a reality.

I often get asked what the best methods of campaigning are. The truth is that there are many different ways and usually it depends on the circumstances. But there are a huge range of options to try. If, in the pre-digital age, there were limits to creativity and campaigning (which I doubt), there certainly aren't today. I'm not a campaigner. Mostly. I suppose that with my organisation, Simple Politics, we're sort of campaigning for better coverage of politics. But it's not the strongest of campaigns, we're just trying to raise awareness for the things we think are important.

So it's a bit of a cop out, but I always say the same thing. One of the first key steps is not so much deciding what method to try, but working out who has the power to change the thing you want to change and how you can influence their decision-making process.

I think the best way, therefore, to find out how to make change happen is to look at a few people who have managed to do just that. Campaigners who started off with a vision and ended up seeing that vision come to pass. They may not have done it alone, but they played a key role. And it worked. Change happened.

You can take what you want from these. Don't forget, we're not looking at arguments. You don't have to agree with any or all of the campaigns. We're just looking at what people did and how they helped the change come about. I think it's also worth saying that these aren't necessarily road maps. These methods worked in these specific conditions and probably won't apply exactly to any other situation, but hopefully there will be ideas you can take away and, if nothing else, they'll be a source of inspiration.

Nigel Farage

We're kicking off with a man whose name you know. You've almost certainly got an opinion of him already. That's all well and good, but I'd ask you to check your bias at the door for this one. Whatever else has happened around Brexit, Nigel Farage has been focused on getting the UK out of the EU for over a quarter of a century, and – unless something very unexpected happens while this book is being printed – he certainly achieved his aim. So let's look at how he went about it.

For starters, we need to know that he is a libertarian. His first job was in the markets, buying and selling at the London Metal Exchange. He's all about freedom and free trade and all that sort of thing.

Sadly, for him, he missed out on the opportunity to vote in the EEC referendum in 1975, because he was only ten years old – I think we can guess which way he would have cast his ballot – but he first signed up to the Conservative Party in 1978. He wanted to get involved.

His love of the free market meant he was no fan of Maastricht and the creation of the EU. He left the Conservative Party in 1992 as a result of John Major's keenness to sign the treaty, and that's when his campaign against the EU started in earnest.

In 1993, he was a founding member of UKIP. This new party knew that the only people who had the power to remove us from the EU were the ones in the government. Farage clearly didn't think he could sweep to power immediately, but he didn't need to in order to achieve his aim. For his campaign to be successful, the people at the top of the ruling party needed to be persuaded, and one way to do that was through the ballot box.

The logic is this: if you build a small party that can take votes away from a bigger party, the bigger party will get worried. If, for example, it looked like UKIP was going to split the Conservative vote in a particular constituency, meaning the Labour Party might win, then the Conservative Party might adopt some of UKIP's policies so as not to lose voters.

Farage first stood for election the following year, in 1994. He didn't do very well, securing just 952 votes – only 169 more than the Monster Raving Loony Party's Screaming Lord Sutch. On the same day, there were elections for the European Parliament, in which Farage was entered. He did better than he had in the by-election, but not well enough to succeed.

He tried again in Salisbury in 1997 and this time did better, securing over 5 per cent of the vote (and therefore keeping his deposit) and coming fourth, miles ahead of the Green Party.

The issue for UKIP at this point was the existence of another anti-EU political party, the Referendum Party, set up by James Goldsmith, which had done better than UKIP in the 1997 election, almost always beating it when they were up against each other. But when Goldsmith died shortly after, UKIP was poised and ready to take over.

Farage had his first electoral success in 1999, when he was one of three UKIP people to be voted in as an MEP. That gave him a platform and, oh boy, did he use it. He first went on BBC's *Question Time* in November the following year. He would go on to equal (with Ken Clarke) the most appearances on the show – thirty-two separate occasions between 2000 and 2018. Clearly his passion and tenacity gave the programme something it wanted. His growing popularity is testament to the way he engages with audiences.

You see, campaigning isn't just about going through the list of methods. It's about playing to your strengths too. Farage has always been something of an extrovert. Over the years, he has shown he has the ability to make political arguments in ways that resonate with people who might otherwise be disengaged. He's an excellent speaker. When he tells an audience that they should be freer, people tend to agree. He drinks and smokes in a world that increasingly frowns upon these things. He embodies a sense of freedom that appeals to many.

It wasn't just on TV he was making waves. Farage had been speaking and debating in public as often as he could, getting out there and banging the drum for an EU referendum. I can personally testify to this, as I was organising a school hustings event for the 2014 EU elections, more for (non-voting) students rather than adults. I put in a request to Farage's office, not really expecting anything. Imagine my surprise when he himself responded saying he'd be up for it. This is a man who was utterly determined and fiercely focused on the prize.

In 2006, he became the leader of UKIP. Earlier in the year, David Cameron had referred to the party as 'a bunch of fruitcakes, loonies and closet racists'. But just eight years later, they would win the EU elections. In that time Farage had gone about doing what he does best: presenting himself as different from the establishment, someone who treasures freedoms and British values. His audience grew and grew and grew. That victory in 2014 was the first time a party that wasn't Labour or the Conservatives had won an election for decades.

The plan to apply pressure to the Conservative Party by tempting away their supporters was working. Now, we're not just talking about taking a few votes away. Nearly four and a half million people had voted for the party. And it wasn't just the voters. MPs and activists were jumping ship too. Both Douglas Carswell and Mark Reckless went across to give UKIP its first MPs. Conservative donor Aaron Banks swapped sides, too, giving UKIP £1 million. The party had officially become a massive headache for David Cameron.

Cameron, who was also facing an anti-EU faction within the Conservative Party, needed to do something. He announced an EU referendum. The rest is history.

So how did Farage do it? He had a single-minded approach to the EU for years and years. Decades. He didn't give up, even though he had some pretty big issues at the start: nobody voted for him, people laughed at his party, leaders departed saying it was all a bit too right wing. None of this deterred him. The opposite, in fact. He gave his absolute all to the cause, continuing to talk to people, in person, on the radio and on TV. He never let go. Change rarely happens overnight. If you believe in something, you have to be prepared to play the long game.

Laura Coryton

Not all campaigns take years and years, and you certainly don't need to be in charge of a political party to achieve your aims. Our next campaigner harnessed nothing but people power to make her change happen, and it's worth saying from the get-go that it was a huge success.

In May 2014, while studying International Relations at Goldsmiths in London, Laura Coryton started a campaign. She wanted the EU to drop regulations that force the UK to charge 5 per cent VAT on sanitary products. Since the UK joined the EEC in 1973, sanitary products have been subject to VAT – a tax on things we buy that aren't 'essentials' – and 5 per cent is the lowest rate that it can be for members of the EU. Coryton didn't have thousands to spend, nor did she have access to lobbyists. But she did see an injustice that she wanted to fight.

She started a petition on Change.org. Now, there are lots

of petitions out there, many of which are for very worthwhile campaigns. It's a competitive market. So Coryton had to make a splash. One of the barriers she was up against was the whole taboo nature of periods. Many people don't even like discussing the topic, or even using the word. Did that put her off? Absolutely not. She called the petition 'Stop Taxing Periods. Period.' It was signed by a massive 320,089 people.

With such a huge swell of public support, it might be assumed that it was the petition alone that made the difference. Coryton herself, though, suggests that it takes much more than that. She told the *Independent* that petitions 'work well to mobilise people wherever they may be in the world and to centralise a campaign'. In other words, they are useful as a background tool but it's the actions they persuade people to take that really make a difference.

When demonstrating, the taboo nature of the topic can actually be used in its favour to attract attention – an element of shock value. While there are daily protests outside Downing Street, the relatively modest sixty-strong demonstration in attendance as Coryton handed in her petition made national news. The *Daily Telegraph*, for example, reported on the event with an article that opened with a chant from the protesters – 'One two three four, don't you tax me anymore. Five six seven eight, tampon tax is out of date' – before going on to comment that this is 'not what you'd necessarily expect to hear sixty women (and two men) chant outside Downing Street'. When the topic isn't something you usually hear people talking about, a gathering of just sixty people, waving sanitary towels and oversized papier-mâché tampons, can make a wave. It doesn't need the weight of numbers to attract publicity.

Another advantage for the campaign was that it was a very obvious injustice to many people. And one with a clear solution. Most things turn out to be quite complicated: homelessness, for example, might be something everyone wants to end, but a petition to do so would not be effective because it is such a complex issue with no clear solution. Certainly not one that everyone could agree on. This campaign, however, simply said that the UK government is charging VAT on sanitary products, VAT is supposed to be on luxuries, sanitary products are not luxuries, the government should drop the tax. That's super clear.

Obviously there will always be some people who disagree. In 2018 – in The Breakdown – no cause can possibly get everyone on board. Some argued, for example, that anything disposable is a luxury and that tax is there to discourage people from buying things that are thrown away. But this campaign really shows that it didn't matter what those people thought. Coryton ran a very slick, very effective operation. She recruited people online, she got media attention and built support in person out on the streets, she got her clear message across in a clear way. So some people disagree? Who cares? Focus on the people that matter.

As noted, Coryton's campaign was an incredible success. In 2015, David Cameron addressed it, saying, 'I wish we could get rid of this . . . [but] there's a problem with getting rid of VAT on certain individual issues because of the way this tax is regulated and set in Europe.' In the same year, George Osborne specifically mentioned the campaign in his budget speech and pledged that all the money raised by the tax would go to women's charities. Fast-forward to autumn 2018, and the EU rules finally changed (a very, very hard thing to make happen) to allow countries to drop VAT on sanitary products. Even Barack Obama spoke out in favour of the campaign. It was a big win.

Finally, for those who are interested, after securing victory Coryton didn't sit back on her laurels. She now campaigns on period poverty, supplying those in need with sanitary products. It's a campaign that's seen support from many universities, companies such as Boots and Procter & Gamble, local authorities and more. It's almost like Laura Coryton is really very good at this whole campaigning thing.

Caroline Criado-Perez

While some people have very specific and individual causes and campaigns, others find themselves campaigning on a number of fronts. Our next change-maker is a woman called Caroline Criado-Perez. She's a campaigner in the field of female representation. She's been involved in a number of issues around the topic – from statues to bank notes to radio interviews.

When we looked at Nigel Farage, we talked about recognising your strengths and knowing how to best use them. With Farage, that was about being confident and outspoken.

Criado-Perez knows words and how to use them, she knows the online sphere and she knows about communication. While I imagine there is little that the two of them agree on politically, like Farage, Criado-Perez is also a very gifted speaker, with regular tour dates around the country. People pay money to see her talk. Remarkable things can happen when a very intelligent and able person sets their sights on a specific issue.

Perez graduated (as a mature student) from the University of Oxford in 2012. By 2013 she was the winner of the Liberty Human Rights Campaigner of the Year and by 2015 she was awarded an OBE. Her book is called *Do It Like a Woman . . . And Change the World*. This is a serious, focused and able campaigner. Let's have a look at what she's done.

In 2012, Radio 4's *Today* programme ran a discussion piece on women's bodies. Not one woman was involved in that discussion. Instead a man was asked to imagine he was a woman. Criado-Perez used this male-only debate about female bodies to publicly criticise the BBC: 'Again and again, the BBC doesn't try hard enough. Seemingly, it doesn't think fair representation is particularly important.' Soon after, Criado-Perez (and a few others) launched a site called The Women's Room, a database for journalists looking for female experts in a particular field, using the *Today* programme example to draw attention to their cause. Again, as with the period tax, Criado-Perez already had a solution to the problem she was campaigning on. When people agreed with her, they had something to focus their energy on. It's an easy call to arms. People can support what she's doing.

It's not just media representation that has been championed by Criado-Perez. In 2013, when it was announced that Victorian humanitarian Elizabeth Fry was to be replaced on the £5 note, the last female face (apart from the Queen, who's on every note) was about to disappear from our currency. I assume I don't need to tell you that Criado-Perez wasn't over the moon about this.

Perhaps a lot of people would be upset by the idea that there would be no women on the 'celebrated person' side of our bank notes, but most of them would shrug, maybe discuss it in the pub, then leave it be. This is what sets the change-makers apart from so many other people. When they see things they don't like, they take action.

And that's exactly what Criado-Perez did. She started to fundraise for a legal challenge and created an online petition at Change.org. She didn't get the hundreds of thousands that Coryton got for the Tampon Tax, but you don't always need those numbers. Instead, she also targeted those in power, garnering the help of nearly fifty MPs. With 35,000 signatories, a number of supportive MPs and the threat of legal action, the story stayed in the public eye and the pressure built on the Bank of England.

In the end, the very first public communication from the new Bank of England chief, Mark Carney, ended with: 'I therefore understand fully the concern that has been raised by you, and many others, about the potential absence of a female character on the series of four Bank of England notes. I believe that our notes should celebrate the diversity of great British historical figures and their contributions in a wide range of fields.' While the official declaration and unveiling of Jane Austen as the new face of the £10 note was some way off, Criado-Perez had won.

We've seen that Criado-Perez uses her passion, her tenacity and her excellent communication skills to great effect. And, of course, these things snowball. You become known as this campaigner who gets things done, so when you start your next campaign, you bring that victory, those contacts and that know-how with you.

In 2016, she turned her attention to statues in Westminster, specifically on Parliament Square, between the Supreme Court and the Houses of Parliament, next to Westminster Abbey. She saw that there were eleven men depicted. Incidentally, one is Winston Churchill, whose face replaced Elizabeth Fry on the £5 note. Anyway. Yes. Eleven men. No women.

What Criado-Perez did next is absolute text-book successful campaigning. She identified who had the power to make the change: London Mayor, Sadiq Khan. She then set about getting support from the public (her petition received over 85,000 signatures), appealing to high-profile supporters (both for their extra influence on Khan, but also for the public support that comes with such names as J. K. Rowling and Emma Watson), as well as MPs and those from within the corridors of power.

The timing was right too. Back in 2016, the Vote 100 celebration of women being given the vote in 1918 was still two years away. Plenty of time to plan, design and construct a statue of suffragist Millicent Fawcett.

To cut a long story short, Sadiq Khan was convinced: 'It's simply not right that nearly a century after women's suffrage, Parliament Square is still a male-only zone, and I'm thrilled that this is soon to change thanks to Caroline's inspired campaign'. In 2017 it was announced that Gillian Wearing would design the statue. Another win for Criado-Perez.

Ajibola and Conrad Lewis

Some campaigners join the call to arms on their campaign because they look out and see injustice. Some, though, have injustice and tragedy thrust upon them. This is not ideological, this is personal.

In 2010, Seni Lewis was in the middle of his master's degree in IT and Business when he became agitated after a night out. His family decided that he needed medical help, so he was taken to A&E at the Mayday Hospital in Croydon. He continued to display erratic behaviour, so was admitted to the Maudsley Psychiatric Hospital, but there were no beds available, so he was taken to the Bethlem Royal Hospital.

His family didn't feel that they could look after him in the state he was in, and therefore it was agreed that he would voluntarily stay at Bethlem. After his family had left, however, police were called to an incident at the hospital.

Seni was forcibly restrained by seven officers. He was sent back to the Mayday Hospital in a coma. Four days later, he was dead.

In the inquest that followed, the jury found 'that there was a lack of communication between police and medical staff, that the restraint was prolonged, disproportionate and unreasonable, that police failed to follow their training to administer basic life support, and that medical staff failed to respond to the emergency.'

Ajibola and Conrad Lewis, Seni's parents, were devastated. They had left their son in what they thought was a safe place. While still grieving, they set about finding out if this kind of thing had happened before, if other people had died due to police restraint. Sure enough, they found that it had. In 1999, a man called Roger Sylvester, who suffered from bipolar disorder, had died after being restrained by six officers at St Ann's Hospital in Haringey. A man called Frank Ogboru – a tourist from Nigeria – also died under police restraint in 2008.

Ajibola and Conrad Lewis, along with other members of the family, set about trying to ensure that this never happened again. They started working with a group called INQUEST, which describes itself as 'the only charity providing expertise on state related deaths and their investigation to bereaved people, lawyers, advice and support agencies, the media and parliamentarians.' With the charity's help, the case maintained its profile and local Labour MP Steve Reed came to hear about it.

He then set about working with the family and the lawyers to draft a Private Members Bill to make changes to the law, in what would become the Mental Health Units (Use of Force) Bill. The idea was to make instances of restraint much more transparent and accountable, by recording its use every time, improving training for staff (including de-escalation methods), publishing clear policies on restraint, and requiring police officers to wear cameras.

With legal support and an MP on board, the family then needed public and expert support, and to start winning over the necessary numbers of MPs to vote for this to become law.

And so it was that Steve Reed created a petition on the 38 Degrees website that would go onto attract 64,765 signatures. Those who signed the petition were then asked to help the cause further by spreading the word. Thousands wrote to their MPs asking for them to support the measures. Over twenty-five mental health charities also gave their backing.

Often, MPs are not given specific instructions on how to vote on private members bills, so the support from both the public and the industry was able to have a huge impact. Even so, it still didn't have the easiest of routes through Parliament. Conservative MPs Philip Davies and Christopher Chope blocked its path on 15 June 2018. The bill returned, though, and on 1 November 2018 the Mental Health Units (Use of Force) Act was passed.

During the debate, Steve Reed paid tribute to both Seni and his parents: 'I have come to know Seni Lewis's parents, Aji and Conrad, very well over the past few years. They are two of the most dignified and inspirational people I have ever met, but they have suffered pain and anguish that no parent should ever have to face.

'When I asked Aji and Conrad what they hoped for after all they have been through, they told me that they do not want Seni's death to be in vain. They do not want any other family to suffer as they have suffered. I say to this House now, and to his parents, that Seni Lewis did not die in vain.

'We can honour his memory by making sure that no one else suffers the way he did, and by making our mental health services equal and safe for everyone. I dedicate this bill to Seni Lewis. This is Seni's Law.'

Finn the dog

OK, I'll admit it, Finn the dog is not, in himself, a change-maker. He didn't get his paws onto Change.org or any other petition site. He didn't introduce any hip-hop collectives at Glastonbury. He didn't even give Andrew Marr an interview. It's like he wasn't even trying.

But he *is* responsible for a huge change. I mean, yes, his handler PC Dave Wardell did have a big hand in it, but it was Finn as the figurehead that engaged so many and really prompted the creation of a new law.

Here's what happened: on 5 October 2016, Finn the dog was stabbed multiple times in the head and chest. The knife also injured his handler, but it was Finn who was left in a critical condition. Happily, the vet was able to treat his wounds and Finn survived.

As he recovered at home, his story spread far and wide. We're a nation of animal lovers, so the picture of Finn with his tummy and head shaved, with staples and stitches holding him together resonated deeply with the public, and local and national press took notice. The country was rooting for Finn to recover. He even started receiving gifts and cards from the public.

By 10 October – just five days after the attack – a petition was up and running on the Parliament petitions website. The issue raised here was that there was no specific offence of attacking a serving police animal – neither dogs nor horses. Campaigners wanted to change the law so these animals would be given the same status as injured officers.

The speed at which it took off is pretty amazing. By the end of the day on 11 October (the day after the petition was posted), 25,406 people had added their signature. The government was going to have to respond – that's just what happens when a petition gets over 10,000 signatures on the Parliament site.

In fact, the speed of the public's response was way ahead of how quickly the government could react. The petition hit the 100,000 mark – which triggers a debate in Westminster Hall (the second debating chamber – see page 124) – by 3 November. Just twenty-four days. And by that stage the government still hadn't responded to the petition.

On 11 November the government finally published its response. It wasn't good news. It said it was 'grateful for the bravery and skills shown by police dogs' and agreed 'that attacks of any sort on police dogs or horses are unacceptable and should be dealt with severely under the criminal law'. However, 'the law already allows for significant penalties to be issued to those who attack animals that support the police.' The government suggested it would review the sentencing guidelines. This just wasn't enough for campaigners.

With any campaign, the going can get tough. Hurdles crop up. But this must have felt like a particularly difficult one for Wardell and the team. In order to get a new law through Parliament, you pretty much have to have the support of the government. The people in government are the ones with the power to make this happen. And they had just said that they didn't think Finn's Law was needed.

One thing that links all these change-makers, though, is tenacity. They simply don't give up. Ever. And by this stage a Westminster Hall debate had been scheduled. These debates tend to be very interesting; the topics have been selected by the public, so tend to be much more the kind of debate you might hear in a pub/dinner party/classroom. In fact, all of the top ten most-read Parliamentary debates of 2018 were Westminster Hall debates. But, usually, nothing really happens as a result. The government will send a junior minister to respond. That's about it.

The Westminster Hall debate happened only three days later, on 14 November. Brandon Lewis, minister for policing and the fire service at the time, was sent to respond. He effectively repeated the government statement of a few days before, again with lots of good wishes to all, but still saying that all that was needed was an adjustment to sentencing.

So, there they were, a month and a few days in, effectively turned down by the people who could make Finn's Law a reality. What did they do? They went back to the people. They developed their online presence, with a dedicated website to go alongside their social media presence. Wardell co-wrote a book about Finn, *Fabulous Finn: The Brave Police Dog Who Came Back from the Brink*. They launched a persuasive writing tool for schools, helping teachers and encouraging students to write to their MP. Finn himself made several trips to Parliament to help lobby MPs. They kept on going.

A year later, Conservative MP Sir Oliver Heald took up the issue and raised it in Parliament, in the actual House of Commons chamber. Eighteen months after the attack, Finn's Law was finally on its way to being passed. It would be a rocky road; on 15 June, Christopher Chope MP vetoed the Second Reading, but on 6 July the Animal Welfare (Service Animals) Bill finally passed its last hurdle in the Commons. In the chamber, Heald shouted: 'At last!' Wardell tweeted: 'We did it! It's time for #Finnslaw'. History doesn't record Finn's own reaction to the news.

Jordan Stephens

This final example is a bit different from the others. It's about someone who already had a profile and then used that platform to campaign and make change happen. I could have chosen many familiar people who have done this. Joanna

Lumley worked hard for the rights of Gurkhas to remain in the UK. David Attenborough made waves (see what I did there?) about single-use plastic. Jamie Oliver had an impact on school dinners. Malala Yousafzai is an international advocate for giving girls access to education.

The person I've chosen to illustrate this sort of campaigning, though, is a man called Jordan Stephens. He's one half of the hip-hop act Rizzle Kicks. He's the Rizzle bit, if you're interested. He started campaigning on the issue of young people and mental health in 2016, particularly focusing on the idea of 'toxic masculinity'.

What is interesting about this is that he's not trying to bring about a change in the law, but a general change in our attitudes. He wants people to talk more openly and to remove the stigma surrounding the topic. It's a social change. That means that, unlike most campaigns, there is no one person he needs to persuade. It's not about the mayor of London or the prime minister or anyone. It's about encouraging the wider public to start having conversations, intimate and personal conversations, and to rethink their approach to masculinity and mental health.

The focus, therefore, is about getting the message out there, and actively leading that particular conversation. And, yes, it really helps if you already have a following. It's not easy to build a platform from scratch. There are lots of different people and issues vying for attention, so to cut through all the noise out there, it really does help to have that platform first.

And so it was that, in 2016, Stephens launched his #IAMWHOLE campaign. The campaign has three clear aims: starting conversations with young people about mental health; educating them on mental health; and encouraging them to share their experiences of mental health. It was a success almost immediately. He later said: 'It blew up, more than I could have expected, genuinely.'

The campaign was supported by Jeremy Hunt MP (minister for health at the time) and was mentioned in Parliament, but the point of this campaign wasn't to get support from ministers, it was to get people talking and to reach out to people who were suffering in silence. In the first year, the campaign reached 121 million people. It turns out that Stephens, as one half of a fun hip hop duo, was the perfect person to front this campaign. He was well-known enough to attract attention, cool enough to have these conversations without being stigmatised and passionate enough to see it through.

Once started, though, the campaign needed to continue. These conversations can't be a one-off – just something we talk about briefly because Olly Murs mentioned it on TV the other day. This sort of change doesn't happen overnight. It takes time to change people's attitudes and requires a long-term sustained approach. Stephens kept going.

In 2017, while continuing with the #IAMWHOLE movement, he also started talking more often about toxic masculinity, about what is expected of men. He did an interview with the *Guardian* in which he discussed his own issues with mental health. His own self-destructive tendencies. He would go on to talk frequently about his personal story.

He told the Culture Trip website: 'I masked a lot of my early depression with substance abuse and chaos. I know that once I allowed for my sadness to work through me it was really tough. Depression does all it can to stop you. My unhealthy side versus my healthy side. It was a conflict. It was a complete internal war.' And the solution? Talk about things with your friends. Open up. It's a clear and simple message delivered in a way that is engaging for his target audience.

Like many campaigns, there are levels of involvement. There was no petition this time (let's not forget he wasn't trying to persuade people in power), but the website gives people the chance to get more involved. There are packs for teachers, parents and carers, there are more individual stories, there is research into the issues. From casually browsing in response to an interview on TV or a video on social media, you are drawn deeper into the campaign. You are transformed from a consumer to an ambassador, ready to spread the word and start more conversations about mental health and toxic masculinity.

The impact Stephens himself had here is that he's cleared the way for you. He's shown that a fun-loving, music-producing, celebrity-befriending man can talk about deeply personal issues and engage with some of the dark things that you may not have spoken about in the past. That means that you just might find it easier to share what you are going through.

All campaigns attract criticism. Some, possibly many, might think that Stephens should 'stay in his lane', make music and shut up about the rest. Or that his platform gives him the privilege of being able to open up with no stigma. We know, though, that no campaign can engage everyone.

Of course, this example is particularly hard to emulate. Most of us don't have this sort of platform already built up. But while that certainly helped Stephens, it's not necessary to make your campaign successful. As I said before, it's more important to work out who you are trying to reach and how you are going to persuade them to support you. And I think the other key message to take away from all the change-makers in this section is how they kept their focus and drive. No matter what obstacles stood in their way, they were determined not to give up on what they believed in.

Extinction Rebellion

While all around were losing their heads about Brexit in 2019, one group stood out from the rest. Extinction Rebellion – or XR – were there to tell us that we are living in a climate emergency of our own making and we need to act now.

They wanted the government to declare a climate emergency, to reduce emissions to net zero by 2025 and to create and be led by a Citizens' Assembly. It's a tough gig. The Conservative government had already committed to being carbon neutral by 2050 and XR's demands simply aren't compatible with the Conservative vision. They are calling for radical change from those who believe in slow reform.

But let's go back a bit. The first steps to XR were made in mid 2018 when over a hundred clever and/or influential people signed a document calling for action. The number is important because they've never had a leader. In their own words, XR is a 'participatory, decentralised, and inclusive' organisation – a principle that allows its members to act in their own way to achieve the XR demands. Sure, they don't have a single well-known figure to take to the Good Morning Britain sofa to chat to Piers Morgan, but they raise media awareness in a different way.

They first called people together in London on 31 October 2018, to hear their 'Declaration of Rebellion'. Over a thousand people came, and the movement was born, right there on the streets that would become their home.

They had clear demands. They had thousands of supporters. They had a government who they knew wouldn't listen. Conventional means weren't going to square that circle. Their solution? Get out on the streets, in bright carnival clothing, and make a fuss. They would be peaceful, but absolutely break the law. Disrupt. Disobey. Yes, they were going to irritate some people, but they argue they're trying to save the world.

XR haven't yet changed government policy. What they have done is raise consciousness – and pressure. They have forced the issue of the climate and environmental emergency up political, social, cultural and personal agendas, while encouraging individuals to take action. Like others in this section, the work of XR is ongoing.

Conclusion

Let's have a look back, before we look forward. We're living through The Breakdown. In a world where communication is almost impossible, people are looking to make a profit out of your sense of injustice, and communities are blighted by an inability to understand where other people are coming from.

Crucially, though, that's no longer you. You can see through the bluster and the fury into what people are really saying. You can listen to someone with whom you completely disagree, and appreciate their point of view, even if you don't agree with it. The great thing about that is you can compare their ideas to yours and respond calmly and logically. Maybe you'll change their mind, maybe they'll change yours. Either way, your interactions with other people can be so much more positive.

With that rather impressive talent in your skill set, you can go forth and make the world look that little bit more how you'd like it to. The campaigners we looked at have been focused, sure, but they've also known how to communicate their message to the people they needed to persuade. We know how hard that can be in The Breakdown. People find it much easier to talk to others who already agree with them. That's no campaign; those people are already on board. But you? You can bring people over to your way of thinking.

Ladies and gentlemen, in short, we've done it. We've broken down The Breakdown. We can go out and be effective campaigners for the world we want to see, but we can do so without demonising and without attacking.

You've got the tools to carry on like this, too. You're empowered and self-aware. Confident in your own opinions and your ability to justify them. Political conversations are more fun that way – it's so much less frustrating when you understand someone else and can see where they are coming from, when you're both willing to listen, not just shout over each other.

The key is not to slip back. Don't allow The Breakdown to swallow you down again, with its warm comforting blanket of gentle reinforcement. Here's a quick guide to keeping your head clear and out of your echo chamber:

Follow lots of different people on social media. This forces you to see lots of opinions with which you don't agree. If you're a big Corbyn fan, for example, that means opening your life to Guido Fawkes. Or vice versa. And don't just follow them, have a think about what they are saying. Why are they taking that line of argument? Why are they presenting that news story in that way? Do they have any valid points to consider? And follow Simple Politics too, of course.

Watch/follow all the party conferences. You never get a better opportunity to see into the heart of a party than at its conference. It's not just the main speech from the party leader, it's the way the whole thing is organised. Who gets to speak from the stage. How the party runs votes. All that kind of thing. You get to see what's really going on with their ideologies and their visions. Give them a go. Challenge yourself.

Listen to podcasts. Podcasts are a brilliant home of echo chambers. People who all agree with each other, chatting for up to an hour about their ideas while often using this safe space to demonise people with whom they disagree. You know, like you used to. Well, what a great way to immerse yourself in someone else's outlook. Pick a few podcasts from different perspectives. Maybe commute with a different ideology every day. Socialist Saturdays? Tory Thursdays?

Talk to people. Famously, you shouldn't discuss religion or politics. That, though, is because you might fall out with people over them. Now you're out of this whole Breakdown thing and you *get it*, you're free to discuss at will. Nothing exposes you to different opinions like striking up a conversation with a stranger in a bar about things that are going on around the world. So do it.

In short – surround yourself with different voices. Keep it fun. And follow Simple Politics.

How It All Works

A look under the hood of UK politics

When I worked at Parliament's Education Service, I always hated taking the visiting young people into either the House of Lords or the House of Commons when they were sitting. What should have been the absolute highlight of the trip so often ended up with us watching some ludicrously technical debate between five people. It had no energy and even less excitement. It was confusing. And oh so tedious.

Now, I'm aware that by now your appetite has been whetted by all this ideology malarkey. You're fired up and raring to get involved. But alas! Our system is a little idiosyncratic. It can be very hard to get to grips with. In short – I don't want you to be put off like the school visitors to Parliament.

So, to help you along with your new-found enthusiasm for UK politics, here's a quick primer on how some of the key aspects work. There's obviously quite a bit more to it (the technicalities run very deep), but we all have to start somewhere.

The constitution

At the start of September, when teachers get a brand-new batch of students, it's not uncommon for the first lesson to be spent coming up with the Classroom Rules. This is a wonderful exercise that is supposed to be about consensual rule-making. A breaking up of the traditional top-down hierarchy.

Instead it's a cynical ploy to use some of the students' initial enthusiasm against them for, literally, the rest of the year. A student might tell you that no one should be wandering around the classroom. You ask if everyone agrees. Of course they agree. Who sits there and says, 'Nah, we should be able to wander around at will'? Nobody, that's who. So, everyone agrees. And then you've got this lovely contract that everyone has signed up to, saying what you can and can't do. If you've all decided that it's OK to have a water bottle on your desk, then it's OK to do that. The teacher can't suddenly turn around and give you detention for having a water bottle on your desk. Equally, if everyone agreed you can't talk while someone else is talking, then you can expect some kind of trouble if you do. These rules set out the relationship between teacher and students. They were drawn up in a consensual, if slightly manipulative, way, so are hard to change.

That's pretty much what a constitution is: the rules that set out the people's relationship with the state, outlining basic rights and rules. It's not the entire history of laws passed by Parliament. It's just the big stuff.

Much like the classroom rules at the start of term, this important document is usually drawn up when a state is first formed. The most famous constitution is possibly that of the USA (probably because of their cultural dominance, not necessarily because it's the best). Anyway, they wrote theirs in 1787, a few years after they'd kicked the British out in the War of Independence. It begins with the words 'we the people' – which has almost exactly the same vibes as the classroom rules. Not a top-down system (like those evil British people they just saw off), but a consensual way of coming together as a group.

So, we get the idea. A big important book that sets out the rules for a country: who gets to make new laws, who gets to decide if something is legal, who watches the watchmen, etc. The constitution tends to be hard to change, to make sure that someone on a manic ego trip can't remove all the checks and balances. It also gives people confidence that their rights can't be shaken up and taken away without warning. They know, for example, they have the right to remain silent when questioned by the police (although people don't seem to 'take the 5th' in American films as much as they used to). It's there in the constitution.

What a great system, huh? One that protects, that everybody is aware of and is semi-permanent.

Well, if you liked the sound of that, I'm sorry to say – and this is a little awkward – that's not what we have here in the

UK. Not even close. No big book of rules for us. No permanence. No way for everyone to know what it says. Our rules have been adapting and growing and changing for centuries. Why? Because we never had a big revolution and started the country again from scratch. We tried a bit of a civil war once, but we didn't really like how it tasted afterwards, so we invited the king back. A different one, to be fair. We'd killed the first one. The point is we never had a group sitting round thinking about this new country called the 'United Kingdom' and what it is we stand for.

What do we have, then? It's called an uncodified constitution (as opposed to a codified constitution, where it's all written down in one place, like the USA). That means our constitution is all over the place, spread around in different areas, which normally fall into these categories: statue law, common law, EU law, authoritative texts, and traditions and conventions.

Statute law is the easiest one. That's the laws that Parliament passes and it's what makes our constitution very flexible. There is nothing that Parliament can't pass a law on. It's a convention that nothing can bind the hands of Parliament. So if members of Parliament want to get rid of, change, screw up, or do pretty much whatever they like to a law that has been passed previously, they can. They make the rules. Except when the EU does. Although maybe by the time you're reading this we won't be under EU regulations any more. Maybe.

Common law is a bit trickier. This is the laws that are

effectively created by the courts according to something called precedent. Whenever a judge makes a decision, that decision is then set in stone and used to guide future judgements, unless Parliament changes the laws that the decision was based on.

So, imagine two people go to the shop to buy some cheese. One is a bit skint that week, so the other offers to buy the Red Leicester. The one that doesn't pay offers to carry the shopping, do the washing up and tell good jokes on the way. A deal is struck. Cheese is purchased, shopping is carried, dishes are cleaned, LOLs are had.

But then? Disaster strikes. The friends fall out. Both make claims on the cheese, but the one who paid for it refuses to hand any over. No deal can be reached. The skint one takes the other to court to get his fair share of Red Leicester, claiming a deal had been reached and now that deal is being broken. The judge can either say that yes, a deal was agreed, even if nothing was written down, and the bag carrier is entitled to half the cheese. Or the judge can decide that the one who paid the money was the rightful owner and can do with the cheese as they please.

The decision the judge makes would then enter common law. Either we would all have more faith in verbal contracts and agreements, or we would have to learn that they don't actually mean anything.

As you can imagine, there is a huge amount of precedent out there. Every time a judge interprets a law, we've got another piece of common law. The range and scope of our constitution gets bigger. Lawyers have one more thing to use when bickering with each other.

If you thought that common law was complicated, you may not enjoy the next one. That's EU law. The treaties we have signed as EU members and legislation passed by the EU combine to give us rights, to clarify the relationship between us and the people that govern us – and the European courts also set precedent that we all have to follow.

As I suggested earlier, by the time this book is published, we may well be free from all EU laws and courts. We may have gone and taken back control. If we have, all the EU laws will have been transferred to UK laws, and we will be well on the way to adapting them to be a bit more British.

Are you having fun yet? Good. Because we've got to the 'interesting bits of paper' section. Or authoritative texts, if you prefer. Over the centuries, various important documents have been created that form key parts of the constitution.

Back in 1215, for example, King John was not being very nice to his barons. You know what it's like. The king wants all the good stuff for himself – soldiers, money, respect, that kind of thing – and he wants to throw people in prison if they annoy him. For ever.

The barons weren't keen on this, so they made a contract that set out a few boundaries, like trial by jury. It was called Magna Carta, which means 'the big charter' (apparently they weren't into creative nomenclature). King John signed it and in doing so he limited the extent of his power and gave the rich people some rights. Not poor people, of course. Obviously the big charter didn't apply to them.

Magna Carta is an authoritative text, and it is still part of our constitution today. Other examples include the Bill of Rights from 1689, which, for the first time, gave Parliament more power than the monarch. There is also a book that lays out all the rules of how Parliament must work. It's always referred to as Erskine May, after Thomas Erskine May who wrote it all down in 1844, and it's a particularly interesting one because Erskine May was just writing down what already happened, effectively turning traditions into constitutional facts. He went on to release eight different updates, so presumably he wasn't delighted with the first draft. It also demonstrates the shifting sands of Parliamentary procedure.

And finally there are the traditions and customs that we follow. Perhaps the most interesting example is the power to go to war. This power used to belong to the king or queen before it was handed over to the prime minister, along with almost all the other powers belonging to the monarchy. Fast-forward quite a few years, though, and Tony Blair shook things up a bit. He didn't want sole responsibility for taking the country to war with Iraq. He wanted the support of Parliament so that MPs would share the load. On 18 March 2003, he held a vote in the Commons in which 412 MPs voted for the motion and 149 voted against. We went to war with Iraq.

Subsequently, it became a bit of a tradition that the prime minister would ask Parliament if it wanted to go to war. Cameron did so in 2013 over Syria. The vote lost and we didn't bomb Syria. That time, anyway. In April 2018, after the Syrian regime was accused of using chemical weapons against its own citizens, there were renewed calls to intervene, explicitly to stop any future use of chemical weapons.

At the time, it was the Easter holidays and Parliament wasn't sitting. There was uproar and outrage. A young man sat in the audience of BBC's *Question Time* screaming and shouting about how the constitution says there must be a vote in the Commons before we can drop a bomb. He was wrong. Just because a vote had been held on recent occasions didn't mean that Theresa May's hands were tied. She could do what she wanted. We bombed Syria.

The British constitution, then, is a little more complicated than that of our American friends. On the plus side, though, it's very flexible. The democratically elected government can adapt things as they like. If they change things in a way the public don't agree with, we can boot them out and vote in a different lot. Who can then change whatever they like. Go democracy!

Elections

Ah, the sweet, sweet smell of democracy. It comes from the Greek words *demos* and *kratos*, which mean 'people' and 'power' respectively. It's a system in which people can decide for themselves how they should be led, what the country should look like and what rules are needed.

There are very few things about which everyone agrees. Like, really, very few. But the idea of democracy is pretty darn popular. We don't want dictators. We want to have a say.

Democracy, then, is something we're all behind. The trouble is, and I'm sure you didn't see this coming, it's just not as easy as it sounds. It throws up all kinds of difficult questions. Who gets to vote? How should they vote? When should they vote? What are they even voting for?

We're going to start by taking a look at what happens at a general election in the UK – the biggest and most high-profile elections we have, determining who the prime minister and government are. They're a pretty big deal.

General elections

Very quickly, then, this is how it works. The country is split into 650 areas or 'constituencies'. Each one has approximately 70,000 voters (although in deepest, darkest Scotland it can be as low as 21,000, while the Isle of Wight has a whopping 110,000).

In each constituency the various political parties put someone up for election. Most areas in England will have candidates from the Conservatives, Labour, Liberal Democrats, the Green Party and UKIP. They may also have independents and/or candidates from parties such as the Monster Raving Loony Party, the Women's Equality Party, the Christian Peoples Alliance, etc. In Scotland, there is likely to be the Scottish National Party and Wales has Plaid Cymru. Northern Ireland does things a bit differently and has its own set of parties, including Sinn Fein, the Democratic Unionist Party (DUP), the Social Democratic and Labour Party (SLDP), the Ulster Unionist Party (UUP) and the Alliance Party.

Each candidate must put up a deposit of £500, which is returned to them if they get 5 per cent of the votes. That's designed to stop people putting themselves forward just to be silly. It doesn't always work, of course, as there are frequently candidates who aim to do just that. For example, a character called Lord Buckethead has stood against Thatcher, Major and May.

With the candidates all in, everyone goes to the polling station on the allotted day and casts their vote. The person in each constituency with the most votes becomes the MP for that area. The party with the most MPs forms the government.

And . . . that's it: 650 mini elections that create the membership for the House of Commons. It's a simple system that ensures every citizen has an MP that represents their area.

But is this system good enough? Is the process truly democratic? Because, well, there are some pretty serious issues at work here. You know those boards they have at construction sites? 'There have been 348 days since the last accident'? If the British election system had one of those boards it wouldn't make great reading. There have been 0 elections since the last time people's votes didn't count. There have been 0 elections since the last time some people's votes counted more than others. There have been 0 elections since the system was last rigged in favour of the big parties.

Here's the problem. The only people whose vote counts for anything are those who voted for the winning MPs. So it would be possible for a party to finish second in every seat in the country but not get a single MP. Not one. Now, like Everton winning a trophy, that's a theoretical extreme. But there are criticisms that the system isn't exactly fair, so let's take a quick look at some stats from the 2017 election:

- The Conservatives needed 43,000 votes per MP
- Labour needed 49,000 votes per MP
- The SNP got 35 MPs on the back of fewer than a million votes – 28,000 votes per MP.
- In Northen Ireland, the DUP got 10 MPs with 300,000 votes – 30,000 votes per MP
- The Liberal Democrats got 12 MPs with 2.4 million votes – 200,000 votes per MP.
- UKIP won nearly 600,000 votes and didn't get a single MP. That's over half a million people who don't have anyone from the party they voted for in the Commons.

You see, this system that we have isn't designed to be proportional. Results aren't supposed to be in ratio to the votes received. It's a majority system that's designed to reflect the different character of each area. It's also designed to ensure that one big, strong party will win, rather than having the vote split between lots of small parties who would need to negotiate (yuck) in order to achieve anything.

Some people have suggested that it would be fairer to reform the system to one of proportional representation – i.e., a system where the percentage of votes matched the percentage of seats. The issue with that, though, is if we moved to an entirely proportional system we would lose all that is good about the system we currently have. There would be no link between individuals and their MP. Regional differences wouldn't be reflected. It would inevitably be more complicated. And the parties themselves would decide who had been elected – if the Labour Party received, say, 280 seats, the top 280 on its list of candidates would become MPs, no matter who the public wanted. It would be impersonal, and it might feel not terribly democratic. And what is literally the point of this system? To be democratic.

There are various alternative systems that have been proposed as a compromise, mostly involving complex fractions and maths that no one can understand. And we all know that compromises are rubbish. If there's something you really want, getting a watered-down version of it can only be frustrating. In NBC's *The Good Place*, Ted Danson's character Michael muses on the existence of frozen yoghurt: 'There's something so human about taking something great and ruining it a little so you can have more of it'. That's kind of how it is with voting systems. We have this great idea then ruin it a little.

Here, I have no answers. Voting systems are all flawed. We love the idea of democracy – and yet it remains very hard to achieve. The most frustrating thing is how close we are. We know the theory, we just can't work out how to put it into practice. It's a lot like the time you were inspired by *Bake Off* and, yeah, it didn't really turn out all that well, did it?

The government

I used to be ace at Nintendo's *Mario Kart*. Well, OK, not ace. I was better than average at *Mario Kart*. What's that? You saw me? Fine. I knew how to play *Mario Kart*. I knew about steering and reversing and accelerating. Even cornering. Which means that when I went go-karting for real and I was asked if I knew what I was doing, I was pretty confident. Absolutely I knew what I was doing. I'm sure you know where this story is going. I didn't know what I was doing. It all went wrong. It is way, way more complicated in reality.

And so it is with the government. Even the idea of forming the government is more complicated than you might think. The easy and short version is this: the party that wins the general election forms the government. Except that's not necessarily true. Here's the truer, if more confusing version: the government is formed by the person who can carry enough votes in the Commons to get things done.

As we've seen, there are 650 seats in the Commons. Not all those MPs vote, though. Sinn Fein doesn't go to Westminster. It is a Northern Ireland party that just isn't big on the whole Westminster thing. Its members are more into a united Ireland. So that's seven fewer MPs to vote. Then there are the Speaker and their deputies, who don't vote on a daily basis, so that's four more out, taking the total of potentially voting MPs to 639. To be absolutely guaranteed to win a vote, you'd need to have 320 MPs on your side.

So, in order to form a government after an election, you need to have the support of roughly 320 MPs or more. If you've got that number from your own party, then that's all gravy. In recent years, though, that hasn't been the case, so people have had to rope in other parties. In 2010, David Cameron and Team Conservative had only 306 seats and needed to form a full coalition with Nick Clegg and Team Liberal Democrats. In 2017 Theresa May managed to get 318, which was still short, but close enough to mean that she only needed a looser agreement with the DUP to get her across the line.

Prime minister

Once you've got the votes, you're off to see the Queen. Officially, it's Her Majesty who asks you to form a government. You say yes and that's it. You're the new prime minister. It doesn't matter whether you only just scraped together the 320 minimum or if you're swaggering about with a Blair-like 418. You're still the outright prime minister.

When you become prime minister, there's no induction course. There's no fuzzy welcome video, featuring a young-looking John Cleese to talk you through the whole thing. My first job was at Argos in 1996. I had to watch three separate training videos before I was allowed to step foot in the warehouse to find other people's shopping. And yet . . . to run the country there are no qualifications, no tests, no residential learning retreats.

All of which brings us back to *Mario Kart*. Being in opposition or being a junior minister can't possibly prepare you for the sheer scale of the role of prime minister. Any other role you've had pales into insignificance. The prime minister is in charge of everything. All decisions taken by the government ultimately come back to them. They make all appointments in government. They oversee all the different departments. They have to stand in the Commons and be accountable for every action the government has taken. It's an isolating role, as Margaret Thatcher said: 'Being prime minister is a lonely job . . . you cannot lead from the crowd.'

In short, the prime minister sets the agenda. There are different ministers in charge of all the various departments (health, education, defence, that kind of thing), but they are all appointed by the prime minister. And can be fired by the prime minister too. So they have to do what they are told. All major decisions are either initiated or at least run through the prime minister's office.

Power-hungry future despots shouldn't apply, though. There are limits to the role. When you're choosing who is going to be in your top team, you've got to think about keeping all the different factions of the party happy. That might mean balancing socialists with Blairites, Remainers with Leavers, dog people with cat people. You've got to make sure that all the MPs, members and even voters feel like they've got a representative at the top table. They've at least got a dog in the fight.

The size of your majority can make this process easier. If you've got more than 400 votes in the Commons, it really doesn't matter if you upset a couple of people. Or even a whole wing of a party. They can vote against you, but who cares? You've got plenty more supporters. If you're down to your final couple of votes, though, and maybe relying on another political party to keep you in power, your ability to ignore the troublemakers is very much limited. It's basically José Mourinho season one compared to Mourinho season three.

Your power is also limited by Parliament. We'll discuss this in the next section, but if the majority of MPs want you out, you've got to go. And if all that takes is a few of your own MPs rebelling (as it does if you don't have many more than 320 votes), this can be a very real threat. You need to keep public opinion on your side. You need to appeal to everyone.

The cabinet

The cabinet is formed of the prime minister's top talent. Every organisation has these people. Senior Management. The ones who have nearly made it to the very top, but haven't quite yet, but probably do want to make it, and might make it soon, but also, most of them won't.

There are twenty-one members of the cabinet, plus the big cheese themselves. They are all the heads of the big departments, so between them they run everything from defence to health to international development, etc. They meet once a week, normally in the cabinet room at Number 10, to discuss the Big Decisions.

These Big Decisions are open to all voices in the cabinet. Anyone can argue any side, however ferociously they want to. At the end of the debate or discussion, though, a decision will be reached, either through a vote or the prime minister will lay down what they want to happen. At that point the whole cabinet has to swing behind the idea and publicly back the decision. If they want to criticise the decision, they need to stand down. This is called collective responsibility.

If you were planning a trip with a group of friends, there might be some disagreement about where to go. New York? Brussels? Minehead? Once a decision has been made, though, you've got to go with it. However much you liked the idea of eating bagels and going to 'Central Perk', the opportunity to ride the Master Blaster at Butlin's has more appeal for the rest of the group. You've got two choices: go on the trip – and don't moan all the way, don't be that person – or don't go. If you don't go, you're out of the group. You can then tell everyone what a terrible group they were anyway, how your group would be better, and if anyone wants to join you in a future group, you can all go and check out the Statue of Liberty and the Yankees.

In 2017/18 Boris Johnson was part of the cabinet but was never a fan of the decisions being made. He would frequently hint that he didn't really like what Prime Minister May was up to. He generally held back, though. When Theresa May announced her Chequers plan for Brexit, there were rumours he didn't like the deal; the following Monday he decided to leave the cabinet and the government altogether, and resigned. After that he liberally stuck the knife in, urging people to 'chuck Chequers', comparing the plan to a 'suicide vest' and calling it 'humiliating'.

Away from cabinet meetings, ministers are responsible for running their departments. While the prime minister and the cabinet will take the very top-level decisions together, the day-to-day running falls to the individual minister. They are given their budget and they work out how to spend it, where cuts can be made and where extra money might be needed. Most of the work they do can be completed without needing a new law from Parliament, but if big changes are needed, it's the minister's responsibility to guide the new law through Parliament.

Junior ministers (& PPSs)

Only the top government ministers are in the cabinet, which means the majority of them aren't. Each department has a number of junior ministers who run specific sections. So, there is the main minister for education, for example, but then several others beneath them – one for schools, another for apprenticeships, another for universities, another for children and families, and even another specific one for the state school system.

Public recognition of the junior ministers isn't great. They don't go on *I'm A Celebrity*. Because they're not celebrities. That said, was Georgia Toffolo? Anyway, most of the public don't know who these people are, so junior ministers don't tend to be in politics for the ego rubs. They do it either because they feel they can make a difference in the role, or because they see it as a stepping stone towards more power and responsibility down the line. I was deputy head of year in a school once. I didn't dream of being deputy head of year. It was all part of a master plan to run the world, or at least the year group, at some point. I'm sorry to tell you, but it didn't go very well. I've never run a year group. Sad times.

There are then a bunch called Parliamentary Private Secretaries, or PPSs. There are roughly forty of them, and they are on the very first rung of the ladder. You don't get paid extra for the role. You get absolutely zero recognition. You are still bound by collective responsibility and have to vote with the government on literally everything. They're appointed by the PM, though, so they do get to be in government, and it does suggest they might have a future in government. So, if that's your thing, you'll love being a PPS.

Whips

You'll notice that this book steers away from the history side of all this. We've got centuries of it, though. If you pay for a tour of Parliament, you'll be regaled with bizarre story after mildly amusing story of obscure happenings and traditions. I hate that stuff. I think it puts people off. It sends the message that this isn't for you. You're probably not posh enough. You definitely don't know enough Latin. That kind of thing.

Rant warning – a lot of people say they hate politics. They say it's boring and I think this is exactly why they feel that way. They see the pomp and ceremony and it looks like it's got nothing to do with them. If we can try to talk about politics in a way that focuses on debate, on the issues, in a way that clearly impacts on people's lives, they won't be bored. Because coming up with and discussing alternative visions for the future isn't boring. It's fascinating and has a meaningful impact. OK. Sorry. Rant over.

So, yeah, I'm all about how the place works, how you can relate to it and understand it.

This term 'the whips', though, does need some explaining. It's a term that's guaranteed to raise smirks from sixth formers but of course it has nothing to do with select bedroom preferences. The origins are perhaps even more niche. It comes from a fox-hunting term.

The Whipper-In on a hunt – often referred to as a whip – has the role of keeping the hounds together and disciplined while they hunt out the fox, and is sent off to find any that go missing. They would keep their eyes peeled for the fox, too, so they could tell everyone it had been seen.

Their role in Parliament isn't all that different. The government has about twenty-five whips across both the Commons and the Lords and it is their job to keep the 'hounds' together. They make sure that MPs vote with their party and don't speak out against the prime minister.

Some say the idea of forcing, or at least pressurising, MPs to vote a specific way is undemocratic. The whips, though, say that most MPs are only elected because they are standing for specific parties. Most voters have never heard of the individuals they vote for. People just put a cross next to the party logo. It makes sense, therefore, for the MP to stick closely to what the party stands for.

If MPs don't do as they're told (and whips can't actually force anyone to do anything), there are a few things that can be done. The most severe punishment, for repeat offenders, is to throw someone out of the party. They will still be an MP, but will now officially be an independent MP rather than, say, a Labour MP. Other tools of persuasion available to whips might be offering the opportunity to serve on a Public Bill Committee of particular interest, better office allocation or even time with a particular minister.

Then there are the darker arts. These are the ones that get the most air time, but there is no way of knowing exactly how much they are used. I'm talking about blackmail. Whips, or so I hear, collect things that the individual MPs wouldn't necessarily want in the papers. Then, when an important vote comes up, potential rebel MPs are reminded of certain things. They then find that they aren't quite such the passionate rebel they once were.

The Opposition

While the government does all this for real, with its ministers making real decisions that will impact real people, the opposition (the second largest political party in the Commons – since 1922 it's always been either the Conservatives or the Labour Party) put together a pretend version of the government called Her Majesty's Official Opposition, or just the Opposition.

Like all the best things that are just for show, the Opposition tend to set themselves up as an exact mirror of the government. They have a 'shadow' cabinet minister for each of the Big Team in the government. They have their own whips. They even have their own PPSs.

The Opposition doesn't make any changes or decisions; what it does is offer an alternative to the nation. It can show how that party would be running things. What it would be doing or prioritising differently.

This can be slightly difficult to picture because, for all its arcane terminology, the government is mostly set out as a business might be: a clear top-down hierarchy, with the buck stopping at the top. And, sure, the Opposition is set out like that too. But, in the real world, a competing business would be set up as an actual business that had to operate for real, not just sit around criticising its rivals. Adidas spends most of its time making stuff and not that much time calling press conferences to tell us all how terrible Nike is. That's a more concrete way to be in competition.

There is only one country, though, so there can only be one government running it. And the Opposition (along with all the other political parties that didn't win the election) can only set itself up as a viable alternative – seizing on opportunities to show what a terrible job the government is doing, but also painting a picture of a better world. Conjuring up a vision for the future as it might be if it was in charge of running this joint.

The government is, therefore, pretty darn powerful. Lucky, then, that there's a whole organisation whose role it is to keep tabs on it. That organisation is called Parliament.

Parliament

Parliament is based in the Palace of Westminster. The Houses of Parliament. When people think of politics, this is what they think of. That nice pointy building by the river with a big clock. I should add here that, yes, the bell is called Big Ben and the tower is called St Stephen's Tower, but anyone who corrects anyone else on this is a douche.

Parliament has three main roles:

1. Make laws.
2. Debate stuff.
3. Keep an eye on the government.

But how exactly does it all work? An excellent question.

Who's who

This is something that we always used to drum into people when I worked at Parliament educating students on school trips. There are three parts of Parliament. Three. Got it? Well done you. Give yourself a clap.

The three (yes, three) parts of Parliament are as follows: the House of Commons, the House of Lords and the Monarchy. Although the Queen actually has very little to do with it. So, in a meaningful, day-to-day way there are actually just two parts of Parliament, the Commons and the Lords.

The House of Commons

The inside of the House of Commons is all green benches – you'll have seen it on the news.

This is where the MPs are, all 650 of them. Or at least the 643 that turn up.

You're only an MP for as long as your area votes for you. If there is an election and you lose? Off you go. Back to the normal world. Some MPs are there for a very long time. At the time of writing, Ken Clarke is known as the 'Father of the House' because he has been there the longest. He was elected all the way back in 1970. That's before the floppy disk and the Post-it note existed. I have no idea how he coped.

MPs are busy because they are the representatives of their constituents, so sometimes they are in the chamber of the House of Commons itself and sometimes they are back in the constituency doing MP things there.

The House of Lords

The House of Lords is very different to the Commons. There are various ways to get a seat here, but most of the Lords have been chosen, not elected. Sounds a bit undemocratic, huh? Well, let me explain the thinking behind it.

All the MPs in the House of Commons are there because they managed to get a load of votes. It would be perfectly possible, therefore, for not a single one of them to be very knowledgeable about, say, science. You know what they're like. All smiles and handshakes, no test tubes and lab coats. Bloody MPs. That's why people are selected to sit in the House of Lords – they are chosen because they know their stuff.

Imagine that a new law is coming through Parliament. It's a vital piece of legislation that's definitely going to have a huge impact on all of our lives. At its very heart is something to do with science that none of the MPs have a clue about. They can ask around but, ultimately, they don't really know what they are voting for. As such, it goes through on the nod and everyone is delighted. If that was the end of the process, or if the next chamber was similarly filled with people without the know-how, then we might be passing laws based on pseudo-science all the time, or rejecting ones that genuinely have the potential to improve lives. We need people on board who can help make these sorts of judgements.

That's where the House of Lords comes in. People have been selected because of their knowledge of all kinds of things. These are some pretty darn clever people and, the theory goes, they're pretty darn useful to have in our Parliamentary back pocket for when we need to flash a bit of expertise.

'Hang on!' I hear you say. 'What do these people have to do with the normal day-to-day bits and pieces that the

Lords do?' That's a reasonable question to ask, but the truth is they aren't there for the day-to-day bits and pieces. They are successful busy people. They (probably) don't care about the tax banding of nursery grounds. So, they don't turn up for those debates.

If something is coming up that they feel their expertise is relevant to, of course they pack a bag, head to London and do their thing. The rest of the time, they don't. Which is one reason why they don't get paid a regular wage. It's possible that there won't be any science laws one year, or even the following one either. So our science-y types might not do anything at all at the House of Lords for quite some time. It would be ridiculous to pay them for not doing anything. It would be especially unfair if some of their colleagues were in every day for six months to look at laws related to their own expertise, and that lot were being paid the same amount.

Lords get paid when they are there. They can claim up to £305 a day. They don't get paid if they don't attend. Some people do say, though, that they just turn up to get paid and don't care about us, the issues or the country, or whatever. The fact is, though, that they aren't doing that. Or at least the vast majority of them aren't. There are approximately 800 members in total. There might be a couple who pitch up to get paid and then go for a lovely long, boozy lunch. But you can see that most of them don't because when there is not much happening in the Lords, they are literally not there.

Another criticism of the selection process is that the House of Lords is full of former politicians and friends of the prime minister. When the current system was introduced under Tony Blair, the appointees were labelled Tony's Cronies, because the political press love a rhyme. Perhaps they have a point here, but at the end of the day, we need experts in politics. All those old cabinet members who fill up the red benches really know how Parliament and politics work. We're better off with that knowledge being used to help make things better.

The selection process is how about 700 of them have ended up there. They're called life peers and they are appointed for life, but it's not hereditary, so their children don't become members.

There are about ninety who are there for more complicated reasons. Back in history, before Roni Size won the Mercury Prize with *New Forms* (that's how we all count dates, right?), there were over a thousand members of the House of Lords who were there because their dads had been members of the House of Lords.

Tony Blair thought that having these inherited peerages knocking about in Parliament just wasn't the way to run a country. He decided to get rid of them. He set about reforming the House of Lords with a two-step process, and in the first step he kept roughly ninety of them. Like you might save the last roast potato of your Sunday roast as a little prize for finishing your plate. He didn't, however, finish the task. That potato never got eaten.

That means that there are still members of the House of Lords who are there, partly, because their dads were there. The ninety we still have today were chosen from within the ranks of the 750 or so hereditary peers: fifteen were elected by the whole of the House of Lords, and the rest were chosen according to the ratio of peers across the different parties. It worked out at forty-two Conservatives, twenty-eight cross-benchers (with no political party), three Liberal Democrats and two Labour.

A small point, and I hate being this irritating, but that does mean that some members *have* been elected to the House of Lords.

The final slot in the Lords is made up of a group called the Lords Spiritual. That's the twenty-five most senior bishops from the Church of England. The Premier League of Bishops if you will. It's not always the same positions, as people cycle round and get promoted, retire, etc.

There we go, that's who's in the House of Lords. Which leaves us with the monarchy. There's just one of her. She's there because her dad was king. She'll be there until she steps down or dies, at which point she'll be replaced by the person next in line to the throne, which at the moment is Prince Charles.

Now we know who's involved, let's have a look at what Parliament actually does.

How laws are made

This is a biggie. It's a huge part of the daily life of Parliament, turning ideas for change into hard and fast laws of the land. Hopefully making things better for us all. So, let's look the journey a government bill takes. (It is possible for ideas from individual MPs, or members of the House of Lords, to make their way through the process, but it's super hard for them.)

As with all journeys, the work starts before the official beginning. Sir Edmund Hillary didn't pitch up at the start of an expedition and then start planning.

Government bills start in individual departments. When the people in that department think they've got a plan, they send out a public consultation to find out what people think, what changes they might like to the idea and so on. In the olden days these used to be published in a book-like format, but now it's done almost entirely online. This stage is called the 'Green Paper' and is entirely optional. The publication of a Green Paper is also no guarantee that a new law is on its way. These are very early days.

Next, they might publish a clear policy document, laying out the plan in detail. There is no formal consultation at this point, but the reaction of the public, the media and campaigning groups often serves as a pointer. This is the point at which Sir Edmund might lay his equipment out in preparation. He's not asking for feedback, but if Tenzing Norgay burst out laughing and walked out the room, he might change his plan a little. This stage, as with the Green Paper, is optional. It's called the 'White Paper'.

Assuming reactions have been broadly positive by this point, the government can then bring the idea to Parliament. This is when it formally becomes a bill. We're at the bottom of Everest at this point. Minions have got all our gear. We're ready to roll.

A bill can start its journey in the Commons or the Lords, usually depending on how controversial the idea is. MPs are very busy, so if it's a pretty basic idea, or it's very convoluted and technical, they like to leave the initial stage to their colleagues in the Lords. But we're going to start our example in the Commons.

To help you get your head around how this all works, we're going to follow an entirely made-up law through the process. We're going to put forward a law to prevent the use of private cars on a Tuesday. It'll promote fitness, help with a cleaner environment and encourage people to explore creative ways to get around. No-car Tuesdays. That's the plan.

First Reading

The journey to making this a law starts in the Commons on a wet Tuesday afternoon. With no big fanfare, the minister for transport stands up in the chamber and reads out the name of the bill – 'Private Cars (Banning on Tuesdays) Bill'. He is then asked when the Second Reading will be and he sets a date for two weeks later. The text of the bill is then released and published, giving everyone involved a couple of weeks to read it, do any research, formulate their arguments, and so on.

Second Reading

This is a general debate on the principles. Not an in-depth examination, but, generally, what do we think about this? Is it a good idea? Are there any problems with the concept?

Clearly, this exciting and new way of thinking about Tuesday travelling would sail through this discussion.

At the end of this debate there is a vote. MPs will either vote 'Aye' or 'No'. What normally happens is that the government (whose bill this is, lest we forget) votes for it while the Opposition (whose job it is to say how terrible the government is) votes against it. Which means it passes, because the government side has more votes than the Opposition side.

Committee stage

Having passed the general debate, it's now time for the line-by-line scrutiny. Time for MPs to get to grips with evidence, research and a systematic approach to understanding the whole thing. In order to do this, a committee (called a Public Bill Committee) of between roughly fifteen and fifty MPs is formed. Crucially, though, the ratio of MPs from the different parties corresponds to that in the main chamber. That means that the government still has a majority of votes in the committee.

Changes can be made to the bill at this point. So, an Opposition MP puts forward the idea that people who live in rural areas might find this Tuesday prohibition a little tricky. They suggest that the rule only applies to people in specified big cities. Unless the government agree, however, any vote on this change will be defeated, because of the numbers. The only hope for the Opposition of defeating or changing the bill is to try to persuade some backbench government MPs to vote against their party.

In 2016, David Cameron's Conservative government put out a bill called the Trade Union Bill. It was deeply, deeply unpopular with Labour and other opposition parties. Cameron, though, had a majority in the Commons and there was nothing that Labour MPs could do. They got very angry, they used the media as much as possible, they made passionate speeches, but at the end of the day, they simply didn't have the votes. The bill passed and is now a law of the land. Labour says it will repeal it when it is in government.

Report stage

Once the Public Bill Committee has made its changes (or not), there is a Report Stage. This is when other MPs can suggest changes to the bill. Again, they don't tend to get through without government support. This is where the whips come into their own. It's up to them to ensure that people vote the way the government wants them to.

Third Reading

Normally very brief, this is a final debate on the whole of the bill. No more changes can be made. Speeches are made that often repeat the issues or benefits that have been referred to throughout the process. So the government continues to paint a picture of wonderful traffic-free Tuesdays in a city where people can finally breathe clean air. Even if they can't really get anywhere they want to be.

At the end of the Third Reading there is a final vote. When the bill passes this hurdle (it is exceptionally rare for a government to lose a Third Reading vote), that's it. The journey through the Commons is done. Sir Edmund has reached Base Camp. Bicycle shops are thinking of investing in new premises.

The House of Lords

Members of the House of Lords then go through a similar process, but there are a couple of differences, not least in the length of time it can take. In the Commons there are strict time limits, but the Lords can take as long as the Lords want. Everyone gets an opportunity to speak.

There are no Public Bill Committees in the Lords either. Instead the Committee Stage takes place in the main chamber (or, occasionally, in the Grand Committee Room – the second Lords chamber). Everyone who wants to be involved can be. What this tends to mean is that the real super-experts in this field self-select themselves to be part of the Committee Stage. Those less committed to the cause, or who see themselves as less vital in this issue, can then come to the Report Stage.

In general, the House of Lords is much more relaxed about making changes. They can't do anything at the First or Second Readings, but after that – during the Committee Stage, Report Stage and Third Reading – it's open to all. Anyone can suggest a change at any point and, if it is popular enough, peers will vote to include it.

The other big difference right now is that, since 2015, the government hasn't had a majority in the House of Lords.

There are more Opposition members than there are government members. So if the Lords get together, there is nothing that the government can do to stop them inserting changes or voting against the bill. In May 2018, the Lords inflicted fifteen defeats on the government in a single bill. It was about Brexit, so passions were running high, but it shows how little the government can do to prevent defeats.

For our bill, the Lords have made a change. They have suggested that people could apply for permits to drive on a Tuesday. Permits would be given to people who need to drive for reasons that are beneficial to the community. It's not what the government wants, but nothing can be done about that at this stage.

Ping pong

We've had two Third Reading votes. Both the Commons and the Lords have said that they like the bill and it should become an Act of Parliament. Except they have both signed off on different versions of the bill. Which is clearly an issue.

So now the bill gets sent back to the Commons, with the change the Lords made. MPs then get the opportunity to discuss that change. They can then decide to take it out, keep it in, or make other compromise changes.

What normally happens is that the government takes any changes out. Let's not forget that they were made in a place that didn't have a government majority, so it generally isn't delighted with the suggestions. You know those fifteen government defeats in that Brexit bill? The government took them all out again in the Commons. Every. Single. One.

So, sticking with tradition, the government whips out the driving permits idea. No watering down of this vision for tranquil Tuesdays.

The Lords then have a bit of a conundrum. They can put their changes back in if they want. They've got the votes and the constitutional right to do so. But that might be a little churlish. MPs are the ones who have been elected. Lords tend to describe their own role as 'asking the Commons to take another look'. Once they have done that, though, many peers are happy to let the bill go through as the Commons wants it to. There will always be some who are vociferously plugging away trying to defeat the government again, but this is pretty rare.

In this instance, the Lords aren't going to reinsert their permit clause. They'll let it go.

Royal assent

MPs are happy. Members of the House of Lords are happy. Or at least not doing anything about their displeasure. They've both voted to accept the same version of the bill. It just has one final stage, which is for the monarch to give it the nod. Since 1701 this has been a formality. It always happens.

This is the stage, then, where it stops being the 'Private Cars (Banning on Tuesdays) Bill' and becomes the 'Private Cars (Banning on Tuesdays) Act 2019'. Its journey has been a success. The flag can be raised at the summit.

Debating

Another role for Parliament is debating things – although this takes up considerably less time than lawmaking. It's an opportunity for the people's representatives (and their expert colleagues) to debate issues of national importance. This can be in response to events unfurling, or it can be to mark particular national days or weeks. Ultimately, there is often not very much concrete action as a result of these debates, but they give publicity to causes and can lead to the government introducing a new bill at some point in the future.

Keeping an eye on the government

It could be argued that everything that Parliament does comes down to this. What is the lawmaking process if it's not making sure the government is making good laws? But this section is about the ways that Parliament keep the government honest and true, away from the rigid structures of the legislative process.

Question time

We've all seen PMQs. You know, that session where everyone shouts at each other, the prime minister avoids answering any questions and viewers all hang their heads in despair? Well, the good news is that there is a version of this every day – but it's a bit more disciplined and better humoured.

These sessions are an opportunity for all non-government MPs (so that includes, say, Conservative MPs who are not in the government) to ask questions of the different government departments. It is a chance to hold the government to account, to check progress against promised successes and to make it look silly if it's taken a wrong turn.

For an even more sedate way of asking questions, MPs can send written questions, which then requires the minister to reply in writing. This can take longer but is an excellent way to get updates on facts and figures. If these facts and figures are displeasing, you can always take them to the media. It doesn't all have to be manners and politeness.

Select committees

These are where a lot of MPs do their best work. Every government department has its own select committee. It's a bit like having your own guard dog, except it's only watching you. And it will bark very loudly if you start doing the wrong thing.

Each select committee chooses a specific thing to look at. So, the Health Select Committee could choose to look at cancer waiting times, or the treatment of those with bipolar disorder, or promotion of healthy eating. Or whatever.

Once it has its topic, it asks the public for submissions. Often this is an open invitation for anyone to write in, but the committee will also ask specific experts to submit their thoughts.

The next stage is to bring in the witnesses. These are people who know what is going on in real life. If it were a committee looking at bipolar treatment, for example, it might call in sufferers, carers, doctors, therapists, family members, nurses and anyone else whose life has been affected by the disorder. As part of these witness sessions, the ministers are often also asked to give evidence on what the department is doing.

Once it has heard from everyone, the committee creates a report that gives an overview of the current situation and then makes recommendations to the government. These recommendations aren't compulsory. The government can just ignore them if it wants. Increasingly, though, the reports are released to the news on what might otherwise be a slow news day. The media then reports them as 'an influential group of MPs' and lays out what they are calling on the government to do. This helps put public pressure on the government to implement the ideas, although ultimately, it's still entirely up to the government whether to take any notice or not.

That's what Parliament does. It's very easy to be swept up in all the process and grandeur of national government and Parliament. They are made up of the people on TV. The ones in the limelight. A whole lot of politics, however, takes place away from Westminster, in your local area.

Devolution and local councils
Over the past few decades there has been something of an appetite for allowing people to make decisions in a more local way. It seems churlish, for example, to force the whole of Scotland to use the same education system as the rest of the UK, when there might be a system that is more suited to the region, that can better reflect what the Scottish people want.

OK, so that's the theory. The truth is, though, that devolution (the transfer of powers to local areas) is complicated. Really complicated. Let's start by looking at the democratically elected institutions for the three of the four countries that make up the UK. Here are the headlines:

- Scotland has its own Parliament
- Wales has its own Assembly
- Northern Ireland has its own Assembly (when they agree on enough to sit)

In an attempt to make politics as complicated as possible, all these institutions have slightly different powers, but there are broad similarities. They all run their own education systems (which is why Scottish people don't pay tuition fees to go to university), their own health systems (which is why all three countries now have free prescriptions, while it costs £9 per prescription in England), and they also have the final say on elections to their institutions (which is why young people in Scotland are able to vote from the age of sixteen).

We see, then, that they have specific powers and they're not afraid to use them.

That is, of course, except in Northern Ireland, where the Assembly has a bad habit of not meeting. In Northern Ireland, politics is deeply divided along the lines of who wants to be part of the UK and who wants to be part of a united Ireland. These divisions are very deeply rooted. In 1998, however, the main political parties all came together to agree on a way of working together in the Assembly. There would never be one side in government and the other in opposition. Instead, there would be a power-sharing agreement. The two biggest parties (Sinn Fein, which wants a united Ireland, and the DUP, which wants to be in the UK) would form a government together.

In 2017, however, this power-sharing agreement broke down. At the time of writing, they still hadn't made up.

Elected mayors

There is also some devolution in England – certain areas directly elect their mayors. The most powerful and biggest of these is London, where the mayor oversees a population of 8.5 million people and a pretty big budget. There are seven other cities and city areas that have a mayor, including Manchester, Liverpool, Birmingham, Bristol and Sheffield.

There are also sixteen smaller areas that directly elect a mayor. Some are within the boundaries of one of the more powerful mayors. So, if you live in Bristol you've got one mayor for the East of England region and then another for the Bristol council area. Double the fun.

Councils

Your local council is responsible for a lot of what goes on in your area: libraries, roads, tourism, school provision, parking, buses, parks, social care, planning, etc. But the thing that people seem to focus on most is rubbish collection. And here we are, ladies and gentlemen. We've gone through how this whole UK politics thing works. We've looked at some pretty big questions. Who can start a war? How can we change the law? What powers do cabinet members have? It isn't until now, though, that we reach the single biggest issue in politics. This is what I hear about across the country when I talk to school students, adults, everyone. What do people really care about? Bins. People care about bins an awful lot.

I like talking about bins too. Bins are a great topic, because everyone wants regular bin collections. But money is tight, and the council will also say that less frequent bin collections encourage people to recycle more. The money, though, gets right to the heart of politics. There is a limited pot of cash and a long to-do list, so what do you prioritise? Bin collections? Social care? Parking? These decisions are hard. How do we decide what's most important to us? By voting. Candidates say what they'll do, we look at their different solutions and vote for the one that we like the most.

So, when we're talking about bins, we're actually talking about democracy. And that's pretty great.

Acknowledgements

Since they first arrived, everything I have done is for my children, Caitlin, Alfred and Felix. They are my inspiration and my hope. I aspire to be the same for them. This book is dedicated to them and, one day, I hope they will read it.

Without the help of the wonderful Katie Braid, these words wouldn't have found their way onto paper. Without her support, love and tea making, this would never have got off the ground.

It was my agent, Charlotte Ateyo, who got the ball moving on this. She approached me at a point when I never thought it might be possible. She made it happen. She's great.

Finally, my parents. Always there, always interested, or at least pretending to be interested. A special mention to my father who helped with research. Whenever I was in need of the finer points of capitalism, he was always happy to sell them to me.

Index